ERASMUS

OF ROTTERDAM

ERASMUS
OF ROTTERDAM

STEFAN ZWEIG

TRANSLATED BY EDEN AND CEDAR PAUL

~~~~~~

NEW YORK

The Viking Press

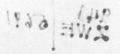

CONTENTS

CONTENTS

ERASMUS

OF ROTTERDAM

I tried to find out whether Erasmus of
Rotterdam was an adherent of that party,
but a certain merchant said to me: "Erasmus est pro se" (Erasmus stands alone).
—*Epistolæ obscurorum virorum*, 1515

AIMS AND SIGNIFICANCE

ERASMUS of Rotterdam, the greatest and most brilliant star of his century, is today, we cannot deny the fact, hardly more than a name. His numerous works, written in an obsolete, supranational tongue (the Latin of the humanists), sleep undisturbed upon the shelves of libraries; hardly a single one of them, though in their day they enjoyed worldwide fame, has any message to our epoch. His personality has been put into the shade by mightier and more imposing reformers, partly because Erasmus's character was difficult to understand, and also because it was full of ambiguities and contradictions. There is little of an entertaining nature to tell of his private affairs; for a man who leads a retired and extremely busy intellectual life scarcely lends himself to description, and is, therefore, a meagre subject for the biographer. But even his actual achievement lies buried and hidden from the eyes of our generation—just as a foundation-stone is concealed beneath the completed edifice. From the outset, that we may get a clear and comprehensive view of the great and forgotten man, I must insist upon the facts that Erasmus of Rotterdam was, of all the writers and creators in the West, the first conscious European, the first to fight on behalf of peace, the ablest champion of the humanities and of a spiritual ideal. The tragedy of his life, and one which binds him to us in closer brotherly affection, was that he sustained defeat in the struggle for a juster and more harmonious shaping of our mental world.

Erasmus loved many things which we ourselves are fond of; he loved poetry and philosophy, books and works of art, languages and peoples; he loved the whole of mankind without distinction of race or colour, loved it for the sake of a higher civilization. One thing alone did he whole-heartedly detest and that was fanaticism, which he looked upon as contrary to reason. He himself was the least fanatical of mortals; it is open to question whether he was a man of first-class intelligence, but no one will deny that he was a man of wide knowledge; his kindliness of heart may not have been overwhelming, but he unquestionably had a straightforward disposition to be kindly; and these qualities combined to make every form of intellectual intolerance irksome to him and led him to consider it as the greatest evil encumbering our earth. He was convinced that nearly all the conflicts arising between men and peoples could be adjusted happily through a little yielding on both sides, since every conflict lies in the domain of the human; and there were hardly any differences of opinion that might not be liquidated satisfactorily were not the area of dispute needlessly expanded. On this ground Erasmus set his face against every form of fanaticism, whether religious, national, or philosophical, considering it as the prime enemy to mutual understanding. He detested bigotry in all its manifestations; he loathed the stiffnecked and the biased, whether these wore a priestly cassock or a professorial gown; he hated those who put on blinkers, and the zealots of every class and race who demanded immediate acquiescence in their own opinions while looking upon the ideas that failed to correspond with theirs as rank heresy or rascality. Just as he himself never wished to impose his outlooks upon his neighbour, so in turn did he refuse to be burdened with the religious or political theories of others if these happened to be alien and unacceptable. He took it as a matter of course that a man had a right to his own opinions; absolute independence of mind was essential. Himself a free spirit, he looked upon it as a fettering of the delightful manifoldness of the universe when, from pulpit or university chair, a man declared his truth to be the only truth, to be a special message which God had whispered into his ear and his ear alone. His life long and with the full powers of his brilliant and incisive intelligence, he fought incessantly against the crazy dogmatism of fanatics, and seldom was he able to smile indulgently over his enemies' vagaries. In these rare and auspicious moments, narrow-minded fanaticism appeared merely as a regrettable sign of intellectual limitation, as one of the many forms of "stultitia" whose thousands of varieties and shapes he made such delicious fun of in his *In Praise of Folly*, where he achieves a most amusing classification. He himself was absolutely fair-minded and incapable of prejudice, so that he could be genuinely sorry even for his bitterest enemy whose foibles he understood. At bottom, however, Erasmus always felt that this ill-omened characteristic of human nature, this fanaticism, would disturb his own spiritual world and the gentle tenor of his life.

For Erasmus's mission, the meaning of his existence, was to bring into a harmonious synthesis all the contradictions which the human brain is capable of entertaining. He was of a conciliatory disposition; or, as Goethe (who had in common with Erasmus, a strong dislike of extremes) phrased it, his was a "communicative nature." Every mighty upheaval, every "tumultus," every clamorous and multitudinous wrangle, was antagonistic to his sense of clarity and reasonableness in the domain of thought. He felt it to be his vocation to fight for universal lucidity. In especial, he looked upon war as the grossest and most powerful manifestation of inner contradictions, and as irreconcilable with his conception of what constituted a moral and reflective man. His greatest asset was that he was endowed with a forbearing disposition which enabled him to exercise the rare art of minimizing conflicts by indulgent understanding, of clearing up ambiguities, of smoothing out confusions, of reuniting what had been rent, of giving back a mutual cohesion to those who were divided. This many-sided desire for conciliation was gratefully recognized by Erasmus's contemporaries, when they coined the neologism "Erasmism" in order to describe it, and it was to "Erasmism" that this one man in all the world wished to lead mankind. Since he united within himself every form of creative activity, being poet, man of letters, theologian, and pedagogue, he considered that even the most disparate entities were capable of fusion; no sphere did he deem unattainable or alien to his arts of persuasion. So far as Erasmus was concerned, there existed

neither a moral nor an unbridgeable antagonism between Jesus and Socrates, between Christian teaching
and the wisdom of classical antiquity, between piety
and ethics. He, an ordained priest, accepted the heathen
into his intellectual paradise; and in the same spirit of
tolerance he took his place side by side with the Fathers
of the Church. Philosophy, so far as he was concerned,
was just as pure a method of the search for God as was
theology, and he did not gaze more reverently into the
Christian heaven than into the Olympus of the Greeks.
Nor did he, as did Calvin and the other zealots, look
upon the Renaissance with its sensual and cheerful exuberance as the enemy of the Reformation, but as the
latter's enfranchised sister. Settled in no country and at
home in all, the first conscious European and cosmopolitan, Erasmus recognized no superiority of one nation
over another; and, since he had disciplined his mind to
estimate each people by the criterion of the noblest and
most cultured of its sons, by its élite, each seemed to
him as worthy of affection as the others. To unite the
men of good will in every land, from every race and
class, in one great league of the enlightened—this sublime endeavour constituted his personal aim in life; and,
since he converted Latin, the supranational language of
his day, into a more literary, more flexible tool for con-

veying thought and comprehension, he thereby created
for the peoples of Europe a means of expression which,
during a moment in the history of human development,
bound them in an intellectual harmony transcending
frontiers. This, indeed, was an unforgettable achievement. His wide vision led him to look gratefully back
into the past; while his trustful turn of mind made him
confidently anticipate the future. But where the barbarism of the world was concerned, the barbarism which
rudely oversets God's plans, which continuously endeavours to destroy the divine ordering of things, to
this barbarism he resolutely turned a blind eye. He was
attracted to the higher sphere, to that which imparts
form and creative activity; and he esteemed it the duty
of every intellectual to widen and extend this realm so
that the radiance emanating from the heavenly abode
might in the end pour down upon the whole of mankind. The fundamental belief of the earlier humanists—
and it was their beautiful though tragical error—was that
the progress of their fellow-mortals could be achieved
by means of enlightenment; and Erasmus, together with
others of his way of thinking, honestly believed that the
individual and the community could attain to a higher
level of culture through the spread of education in
which writing, study, and books were to play the most

decisive part. These early idealists had a touching and devout trust in the capacity of human nature to become more noble by means of the unremitting cultivation of learning and of reading. Erasmus, being a believer in the tremendous importance of printed knowledge, never doubted for a second that good conduct was simply a matter of suitable instruction. The problem as to how human life might attain to complete harmony seemed to him to be elucidated by the humanizing of mankind which he fancied was quite near to achievement.

Such a dream was calculated to act as a powerful magnet attracting the best intellects of the epoch from every land. To men of an ethical bent, personal existence has invariably seemed insignificant and unreal when divorced from the comforting thought, the soul-freeing delusion, that the individual, too, can contribute by his wishes and his deeds towards the perfectionment of the world at large. Each epoch is but a step in the direction of this desired perfectionment; is but a preparation for the better conduct of life. He who on the strength of such a hope fully believes in the possibility of man's moral progress through the birth of new ideals, becomes the leader of his generation. Erasmus was precisely such a man. His concept of a united Europe under the ægis of humanism came at a peculiarly auspicious hour, for the great discoveries and inventions of the turn of his century, the revivifying of science and art by the Renaissance, had brought a fresh and happy current into the collective life of Europe. For the first time after countless years of spiritual oppression, the western world recaptured its sense of confidence in its own mission, so that in every land the finest idealists flocked to the standard of humanism. Each desired to acquire citizenship in the new world of culture: emperors, popes, princes, priests, artists, statesmen, youths, and women vied with one another in assimilating a knowledge of the arts and sciences; Latin became the universal language, an early Esperanto in the realm of intellectual cohesion. For the first time since the break-up of Roman civilization, an all-embracing European culture came into being mainly through the instrumentality of Erasmus and his republic of letters; for the first time national vanity was eclipsed and the wellbeing of mankind as a whole was set up as the goal. And this desire of the educated to bind themselves together in the realm of the spiritual, this wish to create a language which should be a supranational tongue, this longing that peace should be brought to every land by means of an understanding that superseded the individual nations, this triumph of reason over unreason, was Erasmus's own triumph, was his own short and ephemeral but sacred hour in the tale of mankind's years.

Why could not a realm so unsullied endure? How can we account for the fact that these lofty and humane ideals of spiritual understanding, that "Erasmism," exercised so slight an influence upon men who had long since learned to recognize the absurdity of internecine hostility? Thorny questions—but we needs must acknowledge that a sublime ideal has never, so far, fully penetrated to the broad masses of the people, even when such an ideal would obviously advantage the human commonwealth. The average man is under the spell of hatred, which demands its rights to the detriment of loving-kindness; and ingrained egotism drives mankind to seek personal advantage from every new ideal. For the masses, a thing of concrete and tangible utility invariably takes precedence of an abstract good, so that in politics people will rally round a slogan which, instead of awakening enthusiasm for friendly co-operation, arouses a spirit of rivalry, instils an easily comprehended and obvious antagonism against an alien class, an alien race, an alien religious creed. The devouring flames of fanaticism are far more easily kindled by hate than by any other means. The young long to look a concrete enemy in the face, one whose hackles are rising like their own. Hence a supranational and panhuman ideal such as Erasmism lacks that elementary attraction which a mettlesome encounter with the foe who lives across a frontier, speaks another tongue, and holds another creed invariably exercises. The spirit of faction will, therefore, unfailingly reap a victory by appealing to the inexhaustible discontent of mankind and turning it into certain definite channels. In humanism, in Erasmus's teaching, however, there is no room for the passion of hatred; on the contrary, the distant and scarcely visible goal towards which it heroically and patiently strives is formed of an aristocracy of the spirit; and until this goal is reached, the folk of which humanists dreamed, the all-embracing European nation, cannot be compacted into a united whole. Pan-Europa, Cosmopolis, must exist before it can win general allegiance. Idealists as well as those who know human nature, those who believe in the ultimate achievement of unity among men, cannot afford to blink the fact that their work in this cause is perpetually menaced by irrational passion; they need to realize in all humility that at any moment the floodgates of fanaticism may burst open; and, pressed forward by the primal instincts lying at the base of all that is mortal, the torrent of unreason will break down the dams and inundate and destroy everything that impedes it.

Nearly every generation experiences such a setback, and it is the duty of each to keep a cool head until the disaster is over and calm is restored.

It was Erasmus's tragic destiny to live through such a time of storm and stress. He, the most unfanatical, the most antifanatical of men, living at a moment when the supranational ideal was taking a solid hold upon European thinkers, had to witness one of the wildest outbreaks of national and religious mass-passion that history has ever had to relate. In general, those events which we are wont to deem of great historical importance hardly enter the sphere of popular consciousness. Even the huge waves of the earlier wars merely touched the outside margin of folk-life and were confined within the borders of those nations or those provinces which happened to be engaged in them. Moreover, the intellectual part of the nation could usually hold aloof from social or religious disturbances, and with undivided mind contemplate the welter of passion on the political stage. Goethe was such a figure. Undisturbed amid the tumult of the Napoleonic campaigns, he quietly continued his work. Sometimes, however, at rare intervals through the centuries, antagonisms reach such a pitch of tension that something is bound to snap. Then a veritable hurricane stampedes over the earth, rending humanity as though it were a flimsy cloth the hands could tear apart. The mighty cleft runs across every country, every town, every house, every family, every heart. From every side the individual is attacked by the overwhelming force of the masses, and there is no means of protection, no means of salvation from the collective madness. A wave of such magnitude allows no one to stand up firmly against it. Such all-encompassing cleavages may be brought about by social, religious, or any other problem of a spiritual and theoretical nature. But so far as bigotry is concerned, it matters little what fans the flames. The only essential is that the fire should blaze, that it should be able to discharge its accumulated store of hate; and precisely in such apocalyptic hours of human folly is the demon of war let loose to gallop madly and joyously throughout the lands.

In such terrible moments of mass intoxication and sundering of the world of mankind, the individual is utterly helpless. It is useless for the wise to try and withdraw into the isolation of passive contemplation. The times drag him willy-nilly into the fray, to right or to left, into one clique or into another, into this party or into that. No one, then, needs a greater supply of courage than he who would choose a middle course; he must be strong and resolute, denying himself to every party, steadfastly keeping a level head and preserving independence of thought. At this point the curtain rises upon Erasmus's personal tragedy. He was the first German reformer, and I might truthfully say the only one (for the others were revolutionaries rather than reformers), to try and bring fresh life into the Catholic Church by means dictated by the laws of reason. But he who was essentially the far-visioned man of intellect, the evolutionary, had as antagonist in the arena of destiny a man of action, a revolutionary, Luther, an emanation of the dark, daimonic forces of the Germanic peoples. Dr. Martin Luther's heavy peasant fist destroyed at one blow all that Erasmus's delicate penmanship had so onerously and tenderly put together. The Christian and European world was, consequently, hopelessly divided for centuries thereafter, so that Catholic was opposed to Protestant, northerners to southerners, Germans to Latins. At that time only one choice, one decision, was open to the people of Germany and to western civilization: either to be papist or Lutheran, to obey either the power of the keys or the words of Holy Writ. Erasmus, to his praise be it said, remained the only leader of his epoch who refused to take sides. He neither espoused the cause of the Church nor that of the Reformation, for he felt bound to both: to evangelical teaching, since he himself had so long demanded a careful study of Scripture and had done all in his power to make the Gospels available to the people at large; and to the Catholic Church, since in her he saw the last remaining form of spiritual unity standing solid in a crumbling world. To right of him was exaggeration and to left was exaggeration; to right he saw fanaticism and to left; and he, the intractable antifanatic, desired neither to serve one form of excess nor the other. His only master had always been fair-mindedness, and this master alone would he obey. It was in vain that he endeavoured to save the universal heritage of culture and civilization from wanton destruction, remaining as mediator in the middle of the fray, the most dangerous of positions. With his bare hands he tried to mix fire and water, to reconcile this fanatic with that opposing one—to no purpose, for such reconciliations are impossible of achievement. All the greater honour to Erasmus for the attempt. At the outset the two camps could make neither head nor tail of his attitude; he addressed them gently, and each side hoped to win him over. Neither side realized that here was a man who refused to pay homage to an opinion which he considered erroneous, refused to champion a dogma that was alien to his mind, so that each in turn heaped hatred and derision upon Erasmus's head. Because he could not attach himself to either party, he fell foul of both, saying ruefully: "The Guelphs call me a Ghibelline and the Ghibellines retaliate by saying I'm a Guelph." Luther, the Protestant, fulminated curses against him; the Catholic Church placed his books upon the Index. Yet neither threats nor vituperation could deviate Erasmus from his path, and induce him to rally to one party or the other. "Nulli concedo," to neither shall I belong, such was his motto until the end; "homo per se," man as man, with utmost consistency. In Erasmus's estimation, the duty of the artist and the man of intelligence was to act as sympathetic mediator between the politicians and the leaders and misleaders of a one-sided passion; he was to be the man of moderation who worked towards the golden mean. He was not to rally to either standard, but was to stand alone against the common enemy of liberal-minded thinkers—against fanaticism. He was to take his place, not apart from the factions (for the artist, the man of reflective mind, must be sympathetic to all the outlooks of mankind), but above the battle, fighting with equal valour against one form of excess as against another, and against the accursed and unreasonable hate which is universally prevalent.

Such was Erasmus's attitude in his day and time, an

[18]

attitude which his contemporaries looked upon as cowardly, saying that he was a Laodicean and a trimmer. To be quite honest we have to admit that Erasmus did not, as did Winkelried, rush towards the enemy and gather their spears together against his breast to fall pierced through by the hostile army. Such fearless heroism was not in his line. He stood aside prudently, and bent to right and to left like a reed in the storm; he acted thus because he had no wish to be broken, and so that in the interludes of calm he might rise again. Not for him to carry his independence, his "nulli concedo," like a monstrance before him, but to hide it as a thief's dark-lantern beneath his cloak. He crept away into corners and on to devious paths during the wildest outbursts of popular madness; but—and this is what proves of greatest importance—he kept his spiritual treasure, his belief in mankind, intact and brought it safely out of the terrible storm of hate which raged around him; and it was from this tiny flame that Spinoza, Lessing, and Voltaire, not to mention all the "good Europeans" who trod the same road, were able to kindle their lamps. No clansman could have been more faithful to his tribe than was Erasmus, alone in his generation, leal to the whole of mankind. Though he kept aloof from the battlefield, though he owed allegiance to no army, though he was an outlaw and died alone, forsaken by everyone, he retained his independence—he was free.

History, however, is invariably unjust to the vanquished; she does not appreciate men of moderation, men who play the role of mediators, men who act as reconcilers, in a word, humane men. She loves men of passion, the immoderate, the adventurers in the realms of deed and of thought. Thus, in the case of this quiet servitor of the humanities, she has passed him by with her nose in the air. Erasmus takes a back place on the immense canvas of the Reformation. His contemporary reformers play out their destinies to a dramatic end—John Huss was consumed in flames, Savonarola burned (though after hanging) in Florence, Servetus thrust into the fire by Calvin the zealot. Each lived through his hour of tragedy: Thomas Munzer was tortured to death with red-hot pincers; John Knox died prematurely from the hardships to which he had been subjected; while Luther, straddling the German earth with his sturdy peasant legs, declared in defiance of emperor and empire: "Thus can I and no otherwise"; Thomas More and John Fisher were beheaded; Zwingli died on the battlefield, slain by his own compatriots, and his body was subsequently burned, his ashes strewn to the winds. All these are unforgettable figures, valiant in belief, ecstatic in martyrdom, great under the bludgeonings of fate. But in their trail the desolating flames of religious mania spread far and wide; the devastations of the Peasants' War are witnesses to the zealots' misinterpretation of Christ's teaching; the ruined towns, the plundered farmsteads of the Thirty Years' War—the apocalyptic landscapes are clamorous of human unreason and of a refusal to yield. In the midst of this orgy, however, slightly in the rear of the mighty captains of the ecclesiastical warfare, and holding conspicuously aloof from them, the delicate face of Erasmus, faintly tinged with melancholy, gazes at us from the shadows. He does not stand bound to the martyr's stake, his hand is not armed with a sword, nor does passion disfigure his countenance. But his eyes are lifted serenely upward, those blue eyes, so sparkling and tender, which Holbein has immortalized for us, gaze over and beyond the tumultuous passion of his own day into the no less moving epoch in which we live. His brow is shadowed by resignation—ah, how well he knew the everlasting "stultitia" of his fellow-men! But around his mouth plays a gentle smile of certitude, for he, experienced as he was, knew only too well that passion lives for a day in the æons of time and then grows tired and is extinguished. Fanaticism is fated to overreach its own powers. Reason is eternal and patient, and can afford to bide its time. Often, while the drunken orgy is at its highest, she needs must lie still and mute. But her day dawns, and ever and again she comes into her own anew.

A GLANCE AT THE AGE

THE transition from the fifteenth century to the sixteenth was a fateful period in the destinies of Europe, and in its dramatic succession of events is comparable only with the times in which we live. All in a moment Europe enlarged her frontiers so as to encompass the whole earth, discovery followed upon discovery, and within a few years the adventurous spirits of a new generation of mariners achieved what those of previous centuries had passed over out of indifference or from lack of initiative. Dates succeed one another like the minutes on an electric clock: in 1486 Diaz was the first European to reach the Cape of Good Hope; in 1492 Columbus sailed to the West Indian Islands; in 1498 John Cabot discovered Labrador. The world had been enriched by a new continent. Before this, Vasco da Gama, having rounded the Cape of Good Hope, crossed the Indian Ocean to Calicut, opening up the sea-route to Hindustan; in 1500 Cabral discovered

Brazil; in 1519 Magellan set forth upon the most note-worthy voyage, a voyage which was crowned with success—the first voyage man had ever made round the world, the voyage from Spain and home to Spain once more, though Magellan was killed on the journey. Martin Behaim made his "earth-apple," which when it first appeared was looked upon as an unchristianly hypothesis and laughed at as the work of a fool; but in 1490 this globe was recognized as a correct representation of the earth, so that adventurous deeds had given birth to the boldest thoughts. Between night and morning the round ball of our planet upon which man had so long dwelt but which hitherto had been a terra incognita to him, circling unknown through the stellar universe, had become a reality which any intelligent fellow might explore; the oceans, until then accepted as a wide expanse of blue water wrapped in mystery, had become a place of measurable elements highly serviceable to the human kind. European daring all at once found a natural vent in the ceaseless, the breathless race for the discovery of the cosmos. Every time the guns of Cadiz or of Lisbon greeted a homeward-bound galleon, an inquisitive crowd would gather round the harbour in order to learn of freshly discovered lands, to be told about strange birds, beasts, and men, and to be shown these wonders;

with awe they gazed upon the amazing freights of silver and of gold; and into every corner of Europe news was carried informing the peoples that, thanks to the heroism and intelligence of these same peoples, Europe had become the focus and ruler of the whole earth; almost at the same time Copernicus was exploring the stellar universe; and all these fresh items of knowledge spread rapidly (owing to the recently acquired art of bookprinting) into the towns and even into the remotest hamlets. Thus, for the first time in many centuries, Europe achieved a collective life that brought happiness and wellbeing to her peoples. Within the compass of one generation, the fundamental elements of human philosophy, the whole concept of space and time, took on another aspect and another value. The only other epoch comparable with this turn of the century is our own, with its sudden diminution of space and time by means of the telephone, wireless, automobiles, and aircraft, through its abrupt change in the rhythm of life by discoveries and inventions.

Such a sudden enlargement of the physical universe must inevitably exercise a mighty unheaval in the realm of the spirit as well. Each individual, whether he wills it or not, is obliged to think, to calculate, and to live in terms of a new dimension; but before the brain has had time to accommodate itself to these almost inconceivable changes, the emotions have already suffered a metamorphosis, so that the initial reaction of the spirit is a restless bewilderment, partly brought about by anxiety and partly by a confused enthusiasm, with the result that men lose their bearings and kick aside the norms and the forms which hitherto have kept them under control. Suddenly all that has seemed sure and certain becomes a question for inquiry, the things of yesterday appear antiquated and outlived. Ptolemy's maps, which for twenty generations had been looked upon as an irremovable heritage, were, after Columbus's and Magellan's voyages, laughed at even by children; works upon the cosmos, astronomy, geometry, medicine, and mathematics, which for centuries had been studied and accepted as unimpeachable, were cast aside; all that had been was withered by the hot breath of a new era. An end could be made of the endless commentaries and disputations; the ancient authorities could be ignored as though they were discarded idols; the paper castles of the schoolmen fell down, and the panorama was henceforward unencumbered. A spiritual fever for knowledge and science arose because of this colossal transfusion of fresh blood into the European organism, and the rhythm quickened. Developments, which had been

[26]

going ahead at a measured speed, were now goaded on by this fever, to assume the characteristics of a stampede; everything that had hitherto been stationary was set in motion as if the earth had quaked. The ordering of human life which had been carried on unaltered throughout the Middle Ages was shuffled about so that the lowly strata rose or the higher sank, as the case might be: the orders of chivalry disappeared; the towns assumed an importance they had never known; the peasantry were impoverished; commerce and luxury bloomed like tropical vegetation, thanks to the fertilizing qualities of the gold brought over the ocean. The fermentation grew livelier; the social groupings were recast into new moulds, and resembled in a way our own social reconstructions which have followed in the wake of technical developments and brought about a too sudden organization and rationalization. It was one of those moments when man is overwhelmed by the burden of his own creations and needs every iota of his strength if he is to get hold of himself again.

Not a zone of human organization escaped this cataclysm. Even the religious sentiment, that lowest layer of our spiritual kingdom, was searched out and prodded into activity by the events of this turn in the centuries and in the expansion of the civilized world. The Catholic Church had become petrified in its own dogma and like a solid rock had withstood every assault. Obedience, magnificent in the way it imposed itself upon Mother Church's children, had been the seal and legacy of the Middle Ages. The Authority of the Church stood aloft, brazen and puissant; from below the faithful gazed upward for a sign, breathlessly awaiting the holy word; no doubt was permitted to arise in respect of ecclesiastical truth, and should opposition rear its head the Church knew well how to vindicate her power; for a decree of excommunication could break the sword of an emperor, and an uplifted finger could strangle the words in a heretic's throat. Unanimous and humble devotion to Mother Church, implicit and innocent faith, bound peoples and races and classes, no matter how alien and hostile to each other they might be at heart, into one magnificent community. The people of the Middle Ages possessed but one soul, the Catholic soul. Europe rested in the lap of her mother, the Church; sometimes she was lulled by mystical dreams, sometimes she roused herself, but invariably she returned to repose on the maternal breast, and any desire to see truth by way of knowledge and science was contrary to the spirit of the age. But then, for the first time, a feeling of restlessness entered the heart of the European community. People began to ask themselves why, since the secrets of the earth were being disclosed one by one, the divine mysteries, too, might not be elucidated. Sporadically the faithful rose from the knees of her to whom they had lifted meek eyes in reverence; a new courage of thought and questioning entered their being, and side by side with the explorers of unknown seas and continents, side by side with Columbus, Pizarro, Magellan, arose the generation of spiritual conquistadores who resolutely went forth to discover the infinite. The religious mind, which for centuries had been encased in dogma as wine is held inert in a sealed bottle, streamed forth like ether and penetrated the depths of the people as well as ecclesiastical councils. Even the masses wanted to requicken and change the world. Thanks to this all-conquering self-confidence, the people of sixteenth-century Europe no longer felt like tiny specks of dust thirsting after the dew of divine grace, but as the centre of variegated happenings, as strong caryatides sustaining the universe. Meekness and resignation changed into self-consciousness and proper pride; and it was this confidence in its own strength, this release of the senses from age-long trammels, which has acquired the name of the Renaissance. Shoulder to shoulder with ecclesiastical teaching we have, on the same footing, intellectual criticism; side by side with the Church we have the sciences. Another supreme power has been broken, or at least its strength is diminished; the humble and dumb humanity of the Middle Ages has been wiped out, and a new humanity arises which sets about inquiring and investigating with the same religious fervour it has formerly applied to its creed and its prayers. The cloisters which have been the refuge of those who thirst for knowledge yield place to the universities which, in the twelfth century, already begin to vie with them in importance. These become the fortresses of free investigation, sanctuaries for poets, for thinkers, for philosophers, for scientists, and for all who wish to study the workings of the human mind and to lay bare its secrets. The spirit is finding new fields in which to deploy its forces. Humanism endeavours to bring man once more in touch with the divine, without priestly intervention; and gradually there emerges, tentatively at first, and then borne forward by the self-assertion of the masses, the world-shaking movement of the Reformation.

The turn of a century became an epochal event; Europe had for a short space found one heart, one soul, one will, and one desire. In its unity, in itself as a whole, Europe felt itself paramount, and called upon by an incomprehensible urge to bring about further and yet further changes. The hour was propitious: unrest seethed in every land, anxiety and impatience filled every heart, while over everything there loomed a mysterious search for the liberating word which would indicate the goal towards which all were to strive. Now or never was spirit to renew the world.

A GLANCE AT THE AGE

YOUTH IN OBSCURITY

A REMARKABLE symbol for a man who was to become supranational, a genius belonging to the whole world, was that Erasmus had no mother country, no home. In a certain sense, he was born in void space. The name Erasmus Roterodamus was not bestowed on him by his father or his ancestors. It was an assumed name coined from the language of his adoption, not from the Dutch which was spoken habitually around him, but from the Latin he acquired in later days. The date of his birth is uncertain, though there is good reason to suppose that he was born round about 1466. Erasmus himself is to blame for the obscurity in which his early days are wrapped; he disliked talking about his beginnings, for he was not only an illegitimate child but the son of a priest. "Ex illicito et ut timet incesto damnotoque coitu genitus," and what Charles Reade, in his celebrated work, *The Cloister and the Hearth,* narrates concerning the childhood of Margaret Brandt's boy is the sheerest romance. Erasmus's parents died early; and, very naturally, the relatives wished the bastard to be reared as cheaply as possible. Luckily the Church is never loath to take charge of a youngster who seems of good promise. At nine years of age, little Desiderius (more truthfully, the Undesired!) was sent to school at Deventer and later to Hertogenbosch. In 1487 he entered the Augustinian monastery at Steyn, not so much from religious inclination as because that cloister happened to possess the finest library of classical literature the country could boast of. In due course he became an Augustinian canon, having in 1492 been ordained a priest by the Bishop of Utrecht. His years in the cloister do not seem to have been passed so much in saving souls as in reading the classics and in studying the fine arts.

He was much more the scholar than the priest, and it needs a certain effort of the imagination to remember that this independent thinker and writer remained a member of the clerical order until the hour of his death. Erasmus was a master at the gentle art of turning aside from everything that might be unpleasant to him, and he could keep his personal freedom intact no matter what garb he wore or what outward discipline he was compelled to obey. Two popes granted him dispensations, though the pretexts for asking them were the flimsiest. He was thus dispensed from wearing his priestly robe, and, on the production of a medical certificate, was likewise dispensed from observing the prescribed fasts. Also, in spite of supplications, warnings, and even threats, he never for one single day returned to the monastery.

Herein we see one of Erasmus's most salient characteristics: he would not bind himself to anything or to anybody, neither to prince nor churl; even God's service he refused to undertake for long. An inner urge constrained him to remain free and subject to no one. He never whole-heartedly accepted the guidance of those set over him in authority; he did not feel that he owed allegiance to any court, to any university, to any profession, to any monastery, to any church, or to any town. And just as he preserved his intellectual freedom intact, so all his life long did he quietly but obstinately defend his moral liberty of action.

To this fundamental trait, and organically akin to it, must be added another: Erasmus was fanatically independent, though by no means a rebel or a revolutionary. Quite otherwise, since he scrupulously forbore from open conflict, preferring the role of a shrewd tactician and eschewing unnecessary opposition to the powers that be and to any form of mundane authority. He would rather compromise than fight, veiling his independence in preference to combating for it openly. Not like Luther did he doff his Augustinian habit, casting it aside with a dramatic and challenging gesture. No; Erasmus slipped quietly out of his monkish garb when no one was there to spy upon his action, having previously secured the necessary dispensation. Like his compatriot Reynard the Fox, he skilfully eluded every pitfall laid to entrap his independence. Too prudent ever to become a hero, he acquired all that he needed for his personal development by means of his lucidity of mind and his profound knowledge of the foibles of human nature. Perpetually warring on behalf of his own freedom, he won the day, not by courage, but by using the weapon of psychological understanding.

Now, the art of making one's life free and independent has to be learned—and this is a difficult task where an artist is concerned. Erasmus's schooling was both hard and wearisome. Before he succeeded in running away from the cloister he was already twenty-six years of age, and yet for long he had found its restrictions and its narrow-mindedness intolerable. The first test of his diplomatic astuteness came when he made up his mind to leave St. Gregory's without having to break his vows, and, though determined to go, not to run away from his superiors disgraced and compromised. He therefore went to work secretly, and got the Bishop of Cambrai to appoint him as Latin secretary for the journey to Italy this distinguished prelate was then preparing. Erasmus thus became initiated into court life at Brussels, and, in the very year Columbus discovered America, the captive who had escaped from cloistral confinement discovered Europe, the ground for his future activities. As good luck would have it, the bishop postponed his journey, and his protégé secured ample leisure to arrange his days according to his own taste: he no longer was obliged to say Mass; he sat at an ample board and ate the food that suited his delicate digestion; he conversed with men of learning; he set himself to study the Latin classics and the Fathers with passionate eagerness; and busied himself besides with writing his *Antibarbari*. Such was the name of his first book, and it might appropriately have stood on the title-page of all his subsequent works. Without realizing the fact, he had begun the great campaign which was to engage his energies until his death, the fight against ignorance, folly, and traditional presumption. During this lengthy struggle, his own moral code gained precision, and his learning became more extended. After some hesitation, the bishop gave up the idea of going to Rome, so that a Latin secretary was no longer required, and the beautiful days would automatically come to an end: the monk should obediently return to his cloister. But since Erasmus had now drunk the sweets of freedom, he was determined to go on sipping the delightful cup and never desist. He cajoled his patron into sending him to Paris University that he might study for the degree of Doctor of Theology. The bishop granted this request, and gave Erasmus in addition a small pension, whereupon the young cleric departed with his protector's blessing. The prior of St. Gregory's at Steyn vainly awaited the return of his undutiful son. Well, he must get used to waiting, for the years and the decades passed by and Erasmus never went back, for Erasmus had taken leave of monastery and habit and every form of coercion for good and all.

The stipend granted by the Bishop of Cambrai was certainly a meagre one for a full-grown student of thirty, and Erasmus, in bitter mockery, christened his thrifty patron "Antimæcenas." He who had so rapidly acquired his freedom and had grown accustomed to the lavish table of the episcopal household had now to make the best of his more austere quarters in the "domus pauperum" of the notorious Collège Montaigu, whose rigid rules and ascetic discipline together with the severity of its head, the reformer Jan Standonck, were uncongenial to Erasmus's temperament. This celebrated institution was situated in the Latin Quarter, on the Mont Saint-Michel, approximately on the site where the Panthéon stands today. It was a veritable prison-house of the mind, constraining young and eager students in their wish to acquire learning and secluding them from their comrades in the mundane life without its walls. Erasmus writes of this period as a sentence of imprisonment, a period passed in a theological jail, a waste of the best days of his youth. Our scholar, who for his epoch possessed extraordinarily modern ideas of hygiene, complained in his letters of one evil after another: the dormitories were insanitary; the rooms were icy cold and too near the latrines; no one could survive for long in this "vinegar college" without falling sick or dying. The food, too, aroused his criticism: the eggs and meat were foul, the wine was sour. Parasites abounded, so that the nights were a horror. In his *Colloquia* he asks derisively: "Do you come from Montaigu? Then undoubtedly you were crowned with laurels?"—"No, with fleas!" Nor was corporal punishment lacking, and

what Loyola the fanatical ascetic had gratefully en-
dured during twenty years for the good of his soul,
proved highly obnoxious to so sensitive and independent a man as Erasmus. Even the tuition offended his
taste, for he had already detected the smell of decay in
the formalism of the schoolmen, with its Talmudic
flavour and hair-splitting. The artist in him was dis-
gusted, not perhaps so profoundly as was at a later date
Rabelais, but Erasmus despised scholastic methods with
equal intensity, hating their everlasting endeavour to fit
the mind to the bed of Procrustes. "None can disen-
tangle the mysteries of this science, none at least who
has once frequented the Muses and the Graces. All that
you have learned about bonæ litteræ, you must forget,
and that which you have drunk at the fountains of Heli-
con you needs must vomit forth again. I try not to say a
single word of Latin, a single word that pleases or that
may pass as witty, and I am making such progress in this
endeavour that maybe on a day to come they will recognize me as one of themselves." At last illness came to
his aid. This furnished Erasmus with a pretext for escap-
ing from the galleys of Montaigu, which kept mind and
body in chains. Abandoning the idea of working for his
degree of Doctor of Theology, he went away to recu-
perate. After a while he returned to Paris, no longer to

[39]

dwell in the "Collège vinaigre," but in private quarters, where he eked out the episcopal pittance by taking pupils from among the German and English families residing in the capital. The independent artist was coming to birth in the body of the priest.

But at an epoch that was more than half under the influence of the Middle Ages there was no place for a man of independent mind. The estates of the realm were still graded in very definite classes, so that the mundane and ecclesiastical princes, the clerics, the guildsmen, soldiers, officials, handicraftsmen, and peasants, formed groups of individuals separate and apart, and were severely kept from mixing. For the intellectuals, for creative artists, for the learned, for painters, for musicians, no niche as yet existed, since fees in payment of such work as these produced had not yet been invented. A man of intellect had no choice but to find a patron among the ranks of the ruling castes, so that he was obliged to serve a prince or else to serve God. Since art had not yet become an independent occupation, the artist had to seek the favour of the mighty, had to become the protégé of a gracious master, had to hunt up a sinecure here or a pension there, had—until Haydn's and Mozart's day—to be content to sit below the salt and count himself no better than a domestic. If he did not want to starve, he had to write flattering dedications to the vain, frighten the timid by virulent pamphlets, wheedle money out of the wealthy with begging letters. For ever faced by insecurity, through one benefactor or through many, he had to wage incessant and undignified warfare to secure his daily bread. Ten, and maybe twenty, generations of artists lived from hand to mouth in this way, from Walter von der Vogelweide down to Beethoven—who was the first of the great creators to demand his rights as artist and the first to exercise these rights ruthlessly. But to a man of Erasmus's determined and satirical character such outward humility, such apparent acceptance of patronage, did not imply any considerable sacrifice of his proper pride. Early he saw through the illusion of mundane society. Since he was no rebel, he bowed to existing laws without complaint, his only endeavour being to seek ways and means deftly to evade them. But his road to success was a wearisome and inconspicuous one until his fiftieth year; his lot was far from enviable, living as he did on doles from the rich and begging his way as best he might. Even when his hair was grey, he was forced to hang his head and eat the bread of charity. Endless are his dedications, his flattering epistles which form a major part of his correspondence and could well become the textbook of those who should wish to learn the craft of writing begging letters; subtle and cunning as they are to the verge of a fine art. Yet behind this lack of pride—a lack many have deplored—there lay concealed a resolute and magnificent independence of mind. If he paid flattering compliments in his letters, it was that he might more openly unveil the truth in his books. Though he accepted gifts from anyone willing to bestow them, he never put himself up for auction; everything that might make a claim upon him and bind him to a master he thrust aside. Having earned international fame as a man of learning, there were dozens of universities which would gladly have offered him a professorial chair; but he preferred to work quietly in Venice correcting proofs for Aldus's printing-house, or acting as tutor and travelling-companion to sprigs of the English aristocracy, or living upon the bounty of acquaintances, just as long as it pleased him to do these things and never in any case for long at a time. He consistently refused to barter reputation for honours. This obstinate and resolute desire to preserve his cherished independence, this refusal ever to serve anyone, converted Erasmus into a life-long nomad. He was always wandering from place to place, passing through Holland, England, Italy, Germany, and Switzerland. Of all the wise men of his age, he was probably the most travelled, never actually destitute, never wealthy, always (like Beethoven) living "in the air." Nevertheless, this wandering existence was more akin to his true nature than ever house and home could have been. Better for him to be secretary to a bishop for a while than himself to be a bishop for all eternity; better act as counsellor to a prince at so many ducats a year than himself to be the high and mighty treasurer who paid out the allotted salary. A deep-lying instinct drove this man of wide attainments to fight shy of any form of career or position of power. What he needed was to work in the shadows while another wielded power, he himself holding aloof from responsibility, reading noteworthy books within the four walls of a quiet room, writing works of his own invention, to no man subservient, beholden to none—and such was Erasmus's notion of an ideal existence. In the attainment of intellectual and spiritual freedom he wandered by many and devious paths, always with the same end in view: complete independence of thought, the better to pursue his calling and the better to run his own life.

It was during his first stay in England, when in his thirtieth year, that Erasmus discovered his true sphere of activity. Up to that time he had lived in the stuffy atmosphere of the cloister among narrow-minded and plebeian companions. The spartan discipline of the seminary and the intellectual bigotry of the schoolmen acted on his highly strung nerves like instruments of torture. His mind, inquisitive and all-embracing, could not properly develop in such an atmosphere. Yet the gall and vinegar he drank may have been necessary in order to create a thirst in him for far-flung knowledge and freedom, since beneath the yoke of discipline Erasmus learned to hate as unworthy of human civilization everything that savoured of narrow-mindedness, of doctrinaire partisanship, everything that was violent and dictatorial. Because Erasmus of Rotterdam had had personal experience of the worst side of the Middle Ages, because its steel had bitten into his vitals during his cloistral life, he felt impelled to go forth as herald of the new times. One of his pupils, young William Blount, Baron Mountjoy, invited Erasmus to visit England in the spring of 1499. Now for the first time he could breathe freely and happily in the cultured atmosphere his spirit craved. He came to the island in a fortunate hour, when England was basking in the sunshine of peace after the endless warfare between the red rose and the white. Wherever the weapons of battle or of

politics have been laid aside, there on that ground will
the arts and sciences have an opportunity for freer development. Here, again for the first time, the insignificant pupil and teacher, coming straight from the seclusion of the monastery, was to learn that there are certain
spheres where mind and knowledge are the ruling
powers. No one troubled to ask him about his illegitimate birth, or to inquire whether he had said Mass and
pattered off the prescribed number of prayers. The only
thing which interested the people he associated with
was his intellectual calibre, the fact that he was an artist,
that he spoke a fluent and elegant Latin, that he was an
amusing conversationalist. He mixed with the best of
the land and was fully appreciated for what he was
worth. Glad at heart, he made acquaintance with the
amazing hospitality and the noble-minded spirit of fair-
play of "ces grands Mylords," the English, with their
"accords, beaux et courtois, magnanimes et forts," as
Ronsard expresses it. While in this unknown land, Erasmus discovered that there were other ways of thinking
than those to which he had grown accustomed. Although John Wyclif had long since been gathered to
his fathers, the freer theological discussions he had in-
troduced still blew as a fresh current of sweet air
through the colleges at Oxford; here he found scholars

conversant with Greek, a language he had never studied; the finest brains were at his disposal, the greatest men were counted among his patrons and friends. Prince Arthur (who died prematurely in 1502, his place being taken by his brother Henry), asked that the insignificant little priest should be presented to him. For then and always it was to Erasmus's honour, as a sign of the good impression he created, that the noblest men of his time and generation, such as Thomas More and John Fisher, were among his intimates, and that John Colet together with Bishops Warham and Cranmer were his patrons. Our young humanist eagerly inhaled the current of free intellectual air, utilizing this period of hospitality to widen his attainments in every direction, while by associating with the peerage and the circles of aristocratic men and women his deportment and manners were greatly improved. Consciousness of his own powers and the position these procured for him brought about a speedy transformation in the humble seminarist, changing him into a dignified cleric who wore his cassock as though it were a mundane ceremonial robe. Erasmus determined to become a man of parts, so he learned to ride and to follow the hounds; it was due to his consorting with men and women of refinement, nobles, aristocrats, and gentlemen, that Erasmus stood out from among his

German brethren, rough-hewn and provincial in their ways, as a person of distinction and culture. During his stay in England he was in the midst of the political world, was on familiar terms with the moving spirits in Church and Court, so that his alert and penetrating vision gained in breadth and universality. This is what was later to win for him so great a renown. At the same time, he passed through a period of cheerfulness, writing to a friend: "Thou askest me whether I like England? If thou hast ever believed what I tell thee, I prithee believe me when I say that never has anything done me so much good. The climate is agreeable and wholesome, and the like may be said of the land's culture and knowledge; nor is this of a hair-splitting and jejune type; but, rather, is it profound, exact, and along classical lines, includes both the Latins and the Greeks; so that though there be some few things I should like to visit in Italy I have no active longing to go there for the present. When I hearken to my friend Colet, it seems to me that I am listening to Plato himself; and has nature ever produced a kinder, gentler, happier creature than Thomas More?" England, in fact, cured Erasmus of the Middle Ages.

Still, in spite of his affection for England, he never became an Englishman. He returned from his visit freed from trammels, a cosmopolitan and man of the world, independent and universalist in mind. Henceforward he gravitated towards those circles where culture, education, books, and science were dominant. For him the cosmos was no longer divided up into different countries whose frontiers were formed by rivers or by seas; no longer for him did the estates of the realm or races or classes exist. He recognized but two strata of society, an upper, consisting of the aristocracy of the mind, and a lower, plebeian, barbaric stratum which comprehended the remainder of mankind. Wherever books and educated speech, his "eloquentia et eruditio," prevailed, there from this time on he found his home.

So stubborn a determination to ignore any but those who belonged to the aristocracy of the mind rendered Erasmus's personality somewhat vague, and cut the roots from beneath his work. As a genuine citizen of Cosmopolis he was everywhere a visitor, a guest, never assimilating the manners and customs of any specific people, and never acquiring a single living language. During his innumerable journeyings to and fro, he turned a blind eye to all that was peculiar to the country he happened to be traversing. Italy, France, Germany, England, had, so far as he was concerned, only a dozen or so inhabitants each, with whom he conversed in elegant and polished Latin. A town consisted of its library, and he invariably selected the cleanest inns, where mine host received him the most courteously, and served him the best wines. He knew practically nothing save book-lore, possessing neither an eye for paintings nor an ear for music. The works of Leonardo, Raphael, Michelangelo, passed unnoticed before his gaze, and he looked upon papal enthusiasm for the arts as unnecessary extravagance and as mere love of display totally alien to the spirit of the Gospels. He read neither the strophes of Ariosto, nor Chaucer's great works, nor any of the French poets. Latin, alone, was as music in his ears; Gutenberg's printing was the only art he recognized, the only one of the Muses he felt bound to by the ties of kinship, he, the subtlest type of the man of letters, to whom the content of the world was made intelligible through "litteræ," through literature alone. He could get into touch with reality by no other means than through the medium of books, and he certainly had more intercourse with them than he ever had with women. For books he had a great love because they made no noise, were not domineering, could not be understood by the "dull masses," and were the sole privilege of the educated in an epoch when privilege had ceased to play a part. In this sphere he, who was by habit of a thrifty disposition, could act with largesse; and when he sought to obtain money by a dedication he did so uniquely on account of his desire to purchase books, and ever more books, the Latin and Greek classics. Erasmus loved books, not merely for their contents, but also for their material selves, he being the first thoroughgoing bibliophile. He worshipped their form, he liked handling them, he admired their artistic presentation. His moments of sheerest happiness were those passed at Aldus's printing-house in Venice, or with Frobenius in Basle, standing among the workers in the low-ceilinged room, receiving the galleys still damp from the press, setting up with the masters the delicate and beautiful initial letters, running to earth like an expert huntsman with swift and finely pointed quill the most elusive of printer's errors, deftly rounding off a clumsy phrase; to be with books, dealing with them, working at them—this seemed to him the most natural form of existence. Thus Erasmus never lived among the peoples whose lands he travelled through, never shared in their life and activities; he dwelt above them, in the clear, still ether, in the ivory tower of the artist and academician. But from this tower, which was built entirely of books and labour, he gazed forth, keen of sight like another Lynceus, in order to see and to understand clearly and correctly the living life below.

To understand, and to understand better, this was the special pleasure of this amazing genius. Erasmus was not, perhaps, a man of profound mind in the strict meaning of the phrase; he did not think his thoughts out to their logical conclusion, he did not belong to the ranks of the great reformers who endowed the world with a wholly new planetary universe of the intellect. Erasmus's truths are possibly no more than clarifications. Still, if he lacked depth, he compensated this by the width of his vision; if he was not a profound thinker, he was certainly a correct thinker, a clear thinker, and a free thinker in Voltaire's and Lessing's sense, the prototype of those who understand and make others understand, an "enlightener" in the noblest interpretation of the word. He deemed it his natural vocation in life to bring clarity and frankness into the realm of thought. Everything that was muddled antagonized him; he disliked the mystical and the metaphysical; like Goethe, he hated all that was nebulous. Wide horizons lured him, but he was not attracted towards the deep. He never bent over to contemplate the abyss as did Pascal at a later date; not for him the spiritual earthquakes of a Luther, a Loyola, or a Dostoeffsky, those terrifying crises bordering on madness and presaging death. Exaggeration and excess remained foreign to his eminently rational mind. No man of his period was so free from superstition as Erasmus. May he not often have smiled quietly to himself when he witnessed the spiritual contortions and crises of his contemporaries? Savonarola's visions of hell, Luther's panic at the sudden apparition of the devil, Paracelsus's astral fantasies, must have amused Erasmus greatly, since he himself was capable only of understanding and making comprehensible to others that which was universally understandable. His first glance at a problem brought clarity; and whatever his eyes beheld immediately became lucid and orderly. Thanks to this lucidity of his thought-process and his emotional penetration, he became the greatest elucidator, critic, educator, and teacher of his days—not a teacher of his generation alone, but of subsequent generations likewise, for the men of the Enlightenment, the Freethinkers, the Encyclopædists of the eighteenth century, and many a pedagogue of the nineteenth were sib to his mind.

Unfortunately, in everything that is sensible and instructive there lies embedded the danger of a lapse into the humdrum, and we must not indict Erasmus because the Enlightenment of the seventeenth and eighteenth centuries declined into an exaggerated rationalism, since it merely aped his methods while wandering far away from the spirit of his teaching. These wretched pygmies lacked the pinch of Attic salt, that sovereign and refined wit, that pre-eminent independence of thought, which makes his own letters and dialogues so entertaining and so full of literary savour. In Erasmus's writings we find a cheerful humour making the scales even with a more ponderous erudition. He was strong enough to play with his own intellectual potency. Above all he combined a sparkling and yet by no means malicious wit, a caustic yet by no means icy humour, which Swift was to inherit, and which, later, was to become characteristic of Lessing, Voltaire, and Shaw. As the leading stylistic writer of his day, Erasmus possessed the art of presenting certain truths in a racy and brilliant way; with consummate adroitness and genial impertinence he gave the slip to the censorship, so that many a naughtiness escaped the reproving eye; he was in reality a dangerous rebel who managed never to put himself in danger, seeking refuge behind his professorial robes or deftly assuming the fool's motley. For uttering the tenth part of what Erasmus ventured to say and write, others would have been sent to the stake merely because they expressed roughly what he conveyed with the most delicate of rapier thrusts. His books were acceptable to popes and princes of the Church, to kings and dukes alike; they brought, indeed, to their author munificent gifts and the highest honours. Erasmus packed his wares so cunningly that he was able, unbeknownst, to smuggle all the contraband of the Reformation into cloister and court. He was the initiator—along every route he was a pioneer—of that political prose, ranging from lyrical eloquence to the lampoon, of that art of expressing in winged words the needs of the time, which at a later date was to be so splendidly perfected by Voltaire, Heine, and Nietzsche, an art which made jovial fun of principalities and powers, and which proved so immensely more effective than the open and ponderous attacks of other reformers. Thanks to Erasmus, the man of letters for the first time became something to reckon with, a power in Europe which the other powers must take into consideration. And, since he used his power to unite instead of to disintegrate, for the common weal rather than to create rivalries and antagonisms, he has earned our lasting gratitude.

Erasmus was not at the start an outstanding author. A man of his kind needs to be advanced in years before he can influence the world about him. Pascal, Spinoza, Nietzsche, could afford to die comparatively young because they were men of compact intelligence and their thoughts could find expression in the most condensed form. An Erasmus, however, who was a seeker, a collector, a commentator, and a compromiser, could not find his material within himself but had to pick it up in the exterior world. His genius was not intensive but extensive. He was a man of acquirements, a "knowledgeable man," rather than an artist in the pure sense of the term. His ready intelligence made what he wrote seem to be a conversation, easy, expressive, pungent; and he, himself, once declared that the composing of an entire book cost him less effort than correcting one signature of proof. No need for stimulation where he was concerned; his mind worked swiftly and accurately without needing the goad; words came more speedily than his pen could set them down. Zwingli wrote to him: "As I read, it seemed to me that I could hear you speaking, and could see your small and dapper figure moving about before me in the pleasantest manner." The lighter his vein, the more convincing did he become; and the more he wrote, the greater was his influence.

The first of his books to bring him fame was *Adagia*, and it was by chance that this collection of adages was brought together. It coincided with the taste of the learned world of the epoch, and was full of apt and recondite sayings, enlivened at times with telling comment and bracing anecdote. He had been jotting down these maxims for many years and had used them for his pupils' benefit. The work had been published in Paris in 1500, and very soon obtained a wide circulation. It suited a peculiar form of intellectual snobbery which flourished at that time, for Latin was in its hey-day and every man of literary pretensions believed it necessary, in order to prove the excellence of his education, to pepper his letters or his lectures or his speech with Latin quotations. Erasmus's clever selection spared all and sundry the trouble of going to the original sources. No longer need the classics be read and ponderous tomes consulted. When a letter had to be written, the snobs of the humanist movement had merely to lift a sparkling gem from the *Adagia*, and their turn was served. Since intellectual snobs have always been with us, and probably always will be, the work was a best-seller. A dozen editions followed in quick succession, each one improved and added to, so that the volume grew to be double its original size. It circulated in every country of Europe, and soon the bastard's name became so celebrated that Erasmus came into his own.

One single success, however, does not suffice an author. He has to repeat his triumph again and again to show that he possesses gifts sufficient to his vocation and befitting his position as an artist. Such a faculty is not a thing one can acquire by learning, and a writer never knows beforehand whether his next book is going to be a success or to fall flat. Erasmus did not consciously work for success, and each time that it came to him he was surprised anew. His *Colloquia*, a series of dialogues, was first written for his pupils as forms of polite address in the Latin tongue and with a view to facilitating their acquirement of the fashionable language. It was destined to become a textbook in the schools of subsequent generations. He penned his *In Praise of Folly* as a satire, but the book let loose a revolution against all the authorities. When he set to work translating the New Testament from Greek into Latin, adding comments of his own, he brought into being a new theology. A woman, complaining to him of her husband's religious indifference, inspired him to write a book that should bring solace to her mind. In a few days the work was polished off—and it became the catechism of the new, evangelical form of piety and devotion. Without taking aim, Erasmus almost invariably hit the bull's eye. What moves a free and unprejudiced mind

[57]

invariably comes as something fresh and hitherto un-
heard of to those who are caught in the net of tradition;
for he who thinks independently thinks thoughts that
are the best for all and advantage the multitude.

LIKENESS

LAVATER, whose gifts as a physiognomist none will deny, wrote of Erasmus: "He has one of the most expressive countenances, one of the most decisive faces, I have ever seen." The great portrait painters of the day reacted to this "decisive" physiognomy, this "expressive" face, by drawing it over and over again. They valued it as a new type. Hans Holbein has left six portraits of the "præceptor mundi" at various ages; Albrecht Dürer, two; Quentin Matsys, one. No other German has so extensive an iconography as Erasmus. For it was considered an honour to be allowed to portray this "lumen mundi," this "universal man," who had been able to unite into one brotherhood, to rally around the standard of humanistic culture, all the guilds of handicraftsmen practising the various arts. The painters paid homage to Erasmus as their protector, as the champion of the new ethical shaping of their existence, as the new inspirer of their muse; and they presented him on their canvases with all the insignia of this intellectual puissance. Just as the warrior is presented to us in helmet and armour, the noble with his escutcheon and motto, the bishop with his ring and crozier, so is Erasmus presented to us with the weapon he himself discovered: he is the man with the book. He is portrayed amidst an army of books, writing books, creating books. Dürer shows him with an inkhorn in his left hand and a pen in his right, folios and letters around him. Holbein at one time paints him with his hand resting on a book, and symbolically names the picture *The Labours of Hercules*—a clever piece of flattery worthy of Erasmus's titanic achievements; then, again, we see him with his hand on the head of the Roman god Terminus, as though a "concept" had at that very moment taken birth in his brain. Simultaneously with physical exactness of portraiture we are given the "fine, reflective, shrewdly apprehensive" (Lavater) depiction of his intellectual bearing. Invariably we are shown the thinker, the seeker, the self-prober, and it is this which imparts so great a vividness to an otherwise over-abstract countenance.

Were it not for the inner power reflected from his eyes, Erasmus's face, so far as physical contour is concerned, cannot be called a beautiful one. Nature was not

lavish with her bodily gifts when she fashioned this man
whom she so richly endowed with intellectual capacity;
she was thrifty, too, in the matter of vitality and pleni-
tude of life. His body was delicate, his head small instead of being solid, healthy, and resistant. He was emaciated, pale, and listless; no hot red blood coursed
through his veins. Over his sensitive nerves was
stretched a thin, sickly skin, all the sallower because
of his sedentary occupation within the four walls of
stuffy rooms. As the years accumulated upon him, his
skin grew ever more grey and brittle, so that it came to
look like parchment, and was riddled with creases and
wrinkles. What strikes the onlooker most is this con-
stant repetition of a lack of vitality: hair sparse and not
sufficiently pigmented, so that it lies in colourless blond
wisps upon his temples; hands bloodless and transparent
as alabaster; nose so pointed as to look like a bird's beak,
lips too thin, too sibylline; voice, toneless; eyes, in spite
of their luminosity, too small, and veiled. Nowhere do
we see a strong colour glowing, nowhere a full, round
contour in this ascetic and toil-worn countenance. It is
difficult to picture the man as ever having been young,
as riding on horseback, as swimming and fencing, as
joking with or even caressing a woman, as struggling
against wind and storm, as conversing or laughing. The

fine face, a monk's face, dried and pickled, calls up the
picture of closed windows, over-heated rooms, dust
from books, wakeful nights, and arduous days. No
warmth or stream of energy radiates from this cool
countenance; and, as a matter of fact, Erasmus was always cold, huddling himself in wide-sleeved, thick, fur-
lined robes, cosseting himself against the slightest
draught by wearing a velvet skull-cap upon his prematurely bald head. His face is the face of a man who
never lived in real life, but who lived in thought, whose
strength did not reside in his body, but inside the bone-
case of the skull. Helpless when confronted with reality, Erasmus's true vital energies found expression in the
achievements of his brain.

Erasmus's face has meaning for us only through the
aura of intellect which surrounds it. That one of Holbein's portraits which depicts the thinker in his unique
moment of creative activity is an incomparable, an unforgettable work of genius; from all the great painter's
masterpieces, it stands apart; it is, perhaps, the most sat-
isfying presentation in colours of a writer who is about
to translate through the magic of his pen the abstract
idea into the concrete visibility of the written word.
Once we have seen this notable picture, it can never slip
from our memory. Erasmus is standing before his

writing-table, and one feels, to the very marrow of one's bones, that he is alone. His solitude is untroubled, it is absolute; the door in the background is closed against intruders; no one comes or goes within the confines of this narrow cell; but, even if something were happening in his immediate neighbourhood, he would be unaware, for he is in the trance of creation, absorbed, silent, and still. He looks as if he were carved out of stone, so motionless is he; yet on closer inspection this repose is found to be fictitious, for inside the statue there is a very active life, taut concentration of mental alertness, so that the blue eyes blaze with a glow while the delicate, almost feminine hand traces the letters and words which are to convey on to the paper the inner inspiration. His lips are tightly pressed together, his brow is unruffled and serene, his quill seems to glide along lightly and mechanically. Nevertheless a tiny fold between the eyebrows betrays the strain he is undergoing as he sets down his thoughts in well-turned phrases. The immaterial, almost imperceptible frown so near the creative centre of the brain shows how the man is struggling to find the aptest turn of phrase in which to couch the freshly invented adage. Thought, thereby, seems to become a corporeal phenomenon, and one realizes that everything in the man is tense and vibrant, flooded with a mysterious stream of silence. It is amazing the way in which Holbein succeeds in conveying the chemical transformation of energy which gives material shape to a purely spiritual material. For hours on end one can gaze at this picture, and lend an ear to listen to its all-pervading quietude—for, by thus symbolically presenting Erasmus at work, Holbein has immortalized the divine earnestness of every intellectual creator and the invisible patience which is the asset of a genuine artist.

Holbein's portrait gives us Erasmus's quintessential being; through it alone can we come to realize the hidden power lying within the emaciated little body which, like the snail's shell—a burdensome and friable integument—accompanied the thinker throughout his earthly pilgrimage. During the seventy years of his life he was perpetually afflicted by bad health; for what nature had deprived him of in the way of muscle, she had supplied to excess in the matter of nerves. Even as a young man he was neurasthenic; maybe he was hypochondriacal, for his organs were supersensitive. The protective covering of health was too thin to secure him from assault, so that if he was not plagued with one petty ailment, he was afflicted with another—slight, maybe, but undermining. His digestion gave him unceasing trouble; his limbs were often racked with rheumatic pains or with gout; he "suffered from the stone"; every breath of keen air acted upon his delicate constitution like ice upon a decayed tooth; he was sensitive to the slightest change of climate. In almost every one of his letters he complains of not feeling well. In no place did he feel at ease: heat undid him; fog rendered him melancholy; he detested the wind; he shivered in the cold; stove-heated rooms oppressed him and made his head ache; stuffy air gave him nausea. Though he swathed himself in furs and thick woollens, he could not warm his frail body. By no means inclined to pamper his appetites, he was obliged, in order to conserve a modicum of health, to allow himself certain indulgences. He needed to be particular as to what he drank, and the wines of Burgundy were the only ones capable of whipping up his chilly blood into a semblance of warmth. He was obliged to eschew beer, and the vintages of Baden and the Rhine, these latter being too sour for his delicate digestion. An Epicurean by nature, Erasmus fought shy of badly prepared food, his stomach refusing to assimilate indifferent meat, while the smell of fish revolted him. Such constitutional frailty rendered a certain degree of physical comfort indispensable. He needed soft, warm materials for his attire; a clean bed; costly wax candles instead of the usual dip. Every journey he undertook was for him an unpleasant adventure, and what he tells us of his experience of German inns is not only entertaining in the extreme but highly instructive as to the manners and customs of the day. During his sojourn in Basle he had, day after day, to make a detour in order to avoid a peculiarly evil-smelling street, for every form of stench, of noise, of garbage, of reek, of rudeness, and of tumult afflicted his mind as well as his body and wrought his soul up to the pitch of murderous frenzy. Once, in Rome, some friends took him to witness a bull-fight. He was utterly nauseated by the spectacle, declaring: "I have no liking for such bloody sports, they are relics of barbarism." His tenderness of heart made him revolt at any lapse from civilization. In an epoch of gross physical negligence, he was a solitary hygienist and sought to bring into being such cleanliness as he brought into his style as artist and author. His more modern outlook, his more highly strung temperament, made him far outstrip his rougher, thicker-skinned, iron-nerved contemporaries in matters of hygiene and sanitation, thus anticipating the improvements of a later day. His greatest dread was that he should be attacked by the plague, which was raging throughout every land at that time and causing terrible havoc. If he learned that the disease was epidemic in a region one hundred miles away, he shuddered with apprehension and de-camped panic-stricken, no matter whether the emperor had summoned him to a council or the most attractive proposal had been made to him. He felt personally hu-miliated if he found vermin upon him, or pimples, or a boil. This excessive concern regarding illness never left him all his life. Frank, as every practical man is, he was by no means ashamed of avowing that he "trembled at the merest mention of death," for, like all those who are good workers and enjoy the work they do, he was exas-perated when some petty ailment came to hinder him; and precisely because he knew his own weaknesses very well indeed, he took every precaution lest his frail body should betray him. He shunned too generous hospital-ity, was specially attentive to cleanliness, saw to it that his food was carefully prepared, would not allow Venus to lure him into excess, and, above all, refused to have anything to do with Mars, the god of war. As the years passed by, he increased his precautions, modifying his way of living in order to promote the welfare of his age-ing body and thus foster an increase of the repose, secu-rity, and solitude he needed for his supreme pleasure—work. This painstaking adherence to hygiene and moderation, this resistance to the lure of the world of the senses, secured Erasmus from harm, so that, puny and ailing as he perpetually was, he managed to escape the ills from which so many of his contemporaries suffered during one of the wildest and most unwholesome periods in human history. He attained his seventieth year, keeping that which he most highly valued here below: his clarity of vision, and his unassailable freedom.

Such undue frailty, such oversensitiveness of every organ, is not calculated to produce a hero; such a habit of mind and body as that possessed by Erasmus cannot fail to be reflected in the physique; and we need but glance at any of his portraits to realize at once that he was a man unlikely to cut much of a figure as a martial leader in the turbulent days of the Renaissance and the Reformation. Lavater writes: "In his countenance there is no feature to lead one to suspect any unwonted courage or daring." The same may be said of his character. This gentle creature was not made to put up a fight; Erasmus could only defend himself like those small beasts which, when attacked, sham dead or save themselves by protective colouration. But his favourite method of resistance was simply to withdraw into his shell like a snail whenever the tumult raged around him. The safest shelter, then, was his study, behind a barricade of books. Here he deemed himself really secure. We feel what amounts to actual pain as we watch Erasmus's behaviour in hours when great issues were at stake, for whenever an issue became serious he slipped away out of the danger zone. He could never utter a plain "Yes" or "No," but would use the evasive terms "If" or "Insofar," thus baffling his friends and enraging his enemies. Any who should place faith in him as an ally would be pitifully let down. For Erasmus, being one of the great solitaries, could remain faithful to no one but himself. Instinctively he avoided making any decision because by doing so he would feel bound. Dante, the ardent partisan, would probably have placed Erasmus, on account of his tepidness, in that intermediate abode inhabited by those who had been "above the battle in the fight between God and Lucifer":

> . . . that caitiff choir
> Of angels, who have not rebellious been,
> Nor faithful were to God, but were for self.

Every time Erasmus might have acted generously and with devotion, he sneaked away into an attitude of impartiality; for no idea in the world, for no conviction, could he be induced to place his head upon the block, and suffer for what he at heart knew to be true and right. Erasmus was just as much aware of this trait as were his contemporaries. He was only too willing to admit that neither his body nor his soul contained any of the material that goes to make up the martyr. Following in Plato's footsteps he had come to the conclusion that the most essential virtues of man were fair-mindedness and the capacity to yield. Courage, he maintained, played second fiddle. Erasmus showed, however, that he was a man of pluck, inasmuch as he was not ashamed to admit his pusillanimity—and this is a rare thing to find at any epoch. When he was reproached for his lack of bellicose courage, he retorted with a smile: "Were I a Swiss soldier, that might be a warranted reproof; but since I am a man of learning, and need tranquillity for my labours, it harmeth me not." An inimitable justification, and worthy of Erasmus's wit!

He was an inveterate worker; his brain, ceaselessly active, and as indefatigable and tough as his body was weakly, knew not a moment's fatigue, uncertainty, or assault from the earliest years to his dying hour. It invariably worked with a limpid and inspiring energy. Though his flesh and blood were hypochondriacal, his brain was that of a giant on the warpath. Three to four hours' sleep sufficed for recuperation; the remaining twenty hours were passed in ceaseless toil, writing, reading, arguing, collating, correcting. On his journeys he wrote; in the jolting postchaise he wrote; in every inn parlour the table was cleared for his work. To be awake was for him synonymous with being occupied with literary work, and his quill was as though it were a sixth finger to his hand. Ensconced behind his books and his papers, he looked upon events as from a camera obscura, keenly and inquisitively, so that not a pamphlet or an occurrence in the field of politics escaped his notice. Through the medium of books and letters he learned of all that was happening outside the walls of his study. The fact that this vast accumulation of knowledge was acquired indirectly by means of the written and printed word imparts a flavour of the academical to Erasmus's erudition, and gives a hint of abstract coldness to his writings. Just as his body lacked juice and full-blooded sensuality, so do his works. He saw with his mind's eye, not with his living and absorbing organ of sight; but his curiosity and his desire for knowledge embraced every sphere. Like a searchlight, his vision penetrated each problem of life, illuminating it with an equable and compassionate sharpness; his mind was a thoroughly modern thinking-machine of indescribable precision and amazing grasp. There was hardly a sphere of contemporary thought that his searching glance failed to irradiate; restless, exciting, and yet for ever clear, Erasmus's mind acted as the precursor and pioneer of what the minds of a later epoch were to convert into public knowledge. Erasmus possessed, as it were, a divining-rod, with which he discovered the underground springs that his fellows passed by unheeding. With an instinctive flair, he mined for the veins of gold and silver; but, when he had found the lode, his interest in the problem waned, and he left the wearisome task of boring, of cradling, and of valuing to those who should come after. This was his limitation —or, maybe I should be wiser to say: this demonstrated the magnitude of his mental vision. Erasmus lighted up a problem: he never solved one. Just as the coursing blood of passion was lacking in his physical veins, so, in the intellectual sphere, he was devoid of the fanaticism which went to the extremes of moroseness, and the fury of unreasoning partisanship. His universe was one of width rather than of profundity.

It is difficult indeed to pronounce judgment upon this essentially modern spirit, which at the same time transcends all epochs; we cannot measure Erasmus by the scope of his works, rather must we consider him from the angle of how great an influence he exercised. For his soul was made up of many layers, each consisting of a different talent, the whole a sum-total of endowments and yet failing to form a unity. He was at once bold and timid, pushing and irresolute when it came to the final blow, mentally combative, free-living where the heart was concerned, vain as a man of letters and yet humble outside that sphere, a sceptic and an idealist: these manifold inconsistencies and contrasts were loosely combined within himself. His ant-like diligence, his free-thinking theology, his severely critical attitude to the happenings of the epoch, his gentleness as a teacher, his very modest achievement as poet, his brilliance as letter-writer, his sardonic humour, his tender apostle-ship of all that is human—there was room for these antinomies within the wide spaces of his mind, without rendering him oppressed or creating an inner antago-nism, for the greatest of his talents—a capacity for unit-ing that which seemed irreconcilable, a capacity for re-solving opposites—functioned as neatly within his own skin as upon the world without. But so many and so various inconsistencies do not make for unity, and that which goes by the name of "the Erasmic substance" or "the Erasmic idea" was stamped more profoundly and found more concentrated expression among his fol-lowers than in himself. The German Reformation, the

Enlightenment, the unrestricted study of the Bible as contrasted with the satirical spleen of a Rabelais or a Swift; the European ideal and modern humanism—these are thoughts emanating from Erasmus's brain, but are not due to any act on his part. Though he gave the initial impetus, and set the problem a-going, his own movement overtook and outstripped him. Men of understanding and penetration rarely accomplish anything in the world of concrete fact, for clarity and breadth of insight paralyse the physical impact. As Luther declares: "Seldom are good works undertaken with wisdom and prudence; everything occurs unconsciously. . . ." Erasmus was a shining light of his century, others had to furnish strength. He illuminated the way, others had to pass along it. Like all the springs of light, he himself remained in the shadow. Nevertheless, he who opens new paths, even though he does not himself tread them, is as worthy of our esteem as he who is the first to enter the tracks thus indicated for him. Those who labour in the realm invisible, they too have performed a deed.

THE
MASTER CRAFTSMAN

LUCKY the artist who discovers the true medium
whereby to express in the most harmonious
manner the results of his endowments. Thanks to the
chance writing of *In Praise of Folly*, Erasmus found
the medium best suited to his talents. The well-informed
man of culture, the satirical mocker, and the keen
critic who went to the making of Erasmus here rubbed
shoulders in the friendliest spirit of brotherly affection. No other work from his pen enables us to know
Erasmus and to recognize his mastership so finely as
does this, the most famous of his books and the only
one that has wholly escaped the waters of oblivion. The
bolt was shot into the very heart of the period in the
most carefree and playful spirit. In seven days, and more
to relieve his mind than for any other purpose, Erasmus
composed this dazzling satire. But precisely the frivolity
of the undertaking gave the author wings, so that he
flew upward reckless and unconcerned. Erasmus was

already more than forty, and was not only widely read and well practised with his pen, but was likewise a man who had penetrated deep into the human heart. He found it far from perfect, for reason possessed so little power as against reality, and the impulses seemed to him anything but sane. Everywhere he looked, he beheld

> . . . desért a beggar born,
> And needy nothing trimm'd in jollity,
> And purest faith unhappily forsworn . . .
> And art made tongue-tied by authority . . .
> And simple truth miscall'd simplicity,
> And captive good attending captain ill . . .

so that, like Shakespeare, he felt tired of what he saw.

He who has long been poor, who has had to stand in the shadowed gateway of the mighty begging his bread, is apt to become bitter, to be as filled with gall as a wet sponge is with water. He has learned how unjust and foolish are his fellow-mortals, and his lips are at times awry with anger as he smothers a cry of protest and scorn. At bottom, however, Erasmus was not a "seditiosus," he was not a rebel, nor of a revolutionary disposition. Loud and dramatic complaints were not in his line, for he was essentially moderate and cautious. Erasmus had none of that simple and beautiful delusion

which makes a man feel he can at one blow destroy all
that is bad upon this earth. Why, then, asks Erasmus
nonchalantly, spoil one's chances in respect of this
world; single-handed, a man cannot amend its evil
ways; and, apparently, humanity's powers to delude
others and itself are illimitable. Shrewdness advises us
to let things alone; and the wise man will keep his
wonted calm, glancing at this kaleidoscope of fussy and
foolish activity and then pursuing his own road with a
smile of disdain twisting his lips, the attitude of Dante's
"look and pass."

Occasionally, however, even the wise man is be-
guiled into casting a severe and resigned glance into
this whirlpool of stupidity; he must be in happy mood
to be able to do so, and to smile indulgently at all this
folly. Then his ironical smile will throw a searchlight
into the world which will illuminate it and render it
comprehensible. Coming back from Italy in 1509, Erasmus crossed the Alps. During his stay in Italy he had
witnessed the complete religious decay that was rife
within the Church; had seen the pope, Julius II, wishing
to restore the political and temporal powers of the papacy, himself leading his troops to the combat as boldly
as any other condottiere; had known bishops who, instead of living in apostolic poverty, led lives of luxury

and display; had beheld the iniquitous war-lust of the princes who governed this distraught land, and who attacked one another with the voracity of wolves; had looked upon the pride of the mighty, the horrible destitution among the common people. Yes, he had, indeed, gazed long and distressfully down into the abysmal depths of paradoxical absurdity. Now that lay behind him like a black cloud upon the sunny horizon of the Alps. Erasmus the learned, the bookworm, was a-horse; no longer, thanks be, did he drag a load of literary luggage in his rear, none of the codices and parchments which he delighted in commenting upon went with him on this journey. His mind was free to wanton in the free air, he wanted to play and give vent to his high spirits. Chance, bright and bewitching as a butterfly, passed by and accompanied him for the remainder of this fortunate journey. Hardly had he settled down in Thomas More's cheerful mansion, when he began to write his witty little squib, mainly to entertain the circle of his friends. He christened his satire, in honour of More, with the play on words, *Moriæ encomium* (in Latin "Laus stultitiæ," which is perhaps most happily translated "In Praise of Folly").

Compared with his serious, influential, rather ponderous and highly scientific works, this small book, so full of impudence and ridicule, would seem to have been the outcome of youthful exuberance, a creature light of foot and willowy in figure. But a work of art does not need scope and weight to give it spiritual consistency; and just as in politics one word, one joke, may often have greater effect than the most eloquent speech of a Demosthenes, so in the realm of literature it is not bulk that counts but content. Among the hundred and eighty tomes bequeathed to us by Voltaire, *Candide*, that terse and mocking nouvelle, is the only one to survive hardily and remain of vital interest. So also, among the innumerable folios written by Erasmus's ready pen, this brilliant and spirited *Laus stultitiæ*, the child of a fortunate hour, is the one which still continues to amuse and edify us.

The masquerade Erasmus here depicts with such masterly art is unique, and never again was its author to recapture the genial humour with which it is presented. Erasmus does not in his own person utter the words which convey the bitter truths aimed at the mighty; he places Stultitia, Folly, in the pulpit, and from thence she eulogizes herself. An amusing quid-pro-quo is thus created, for the reader is never quite sure who is talking: Is Erasmus speaking seriously, or is Folly, to whom the roughest and most impudent behaviour may be permitted, giving us a taste of her tongue? By assuming this ambiguous position, Erasmus renders himself unassailable and can permit himself to be as bold as he chooses. His personal opinion is never divulged, and should anyone fancy he can reproach the author for some peculiarly biting observation, or for the gibes which are lavishly sprinkled upon every page, Erasmus has it in his power to reply: "I never said anything of the kind. It was Dame Stultitia that spoke—and who is likely to take the words of a fool seriously?" Criticism of the manners and customs of an epoch when the censorship and the Inquisition flourished was here smuggled into the world by means of irony and symbolism—and this was the only way in which it would have been possible to convey the truth at a time when intellectual darkness prevailed. Seldom, however, has the sacred light of the Fool been more deftly utilized than by Erasmus. In this witty satire his tongue could speak freely, so that *In Praise of Folly* was the most daring and at the same time most artistic work of Erasmus's generation. Earnestness and merriment, profound knowledge and the most impish nonsense, truth and exaggeration, make up the brightly hued mosaic; if the reader should think to catch one mood and examine it, he will find it has slipped from his grasp with a quirk and a prank. If one recalls the style in which most authors of that day expressed themselves, if one remembers the coarse invective with which controversy was carried on, one can well understand why such a brilliant firework, thrown into the midst of the intellectual gloom that reigned, could delight and emancipate the mind for a hundred years after it was concocted.

The satire begins with a jest. Dame Stultitia, in her academic gown but wearing the fool's cap on her head (it is thus that Holbein depicted her), mounts the rostrum and holds forth in praise of herself. She alone, we learn, with her hand-maidens Flattery and Self-Love, keeps the world a-going. Without my aid, no league, no community life, can be a lasting acquirement; were it not for me the folk would not remain loyal to its ruling prince, the servant would rise against his master and the lady's maid against her mistress; the pupil would rebel against his teacher, the friend forsake his friend, the wife desert her husband, the host cheat his guest, one comrade would play his fellow-comrade false; indeed, no man would be able to tolerate another if they did not mutually deceive one another, now by flattery and now by a crafty surrender; in a word, mankind would find life intolerable were it not accompanied by a deep-rooted folly. The merchant goes about his business because of an exaggerated value set upon money; the poet, inspired by the hope of achieving celebrity, creates his work lured by the craving for a spurious immortality; the warrior is courageous because of his illusions of greatness. A sober and right-minded man would take to his heels at the outset of the fray, he would economize his energies and just give out enough to earn a livelihood; were it not for the foolish weed of a wish for immortality implanted in him, he would never raise a hand or exercise his mind. Now a flood of paradox is poured forth in sprightly vein. She, Stultitia, puts blinkers on us all, and she alone is capable of making mankind content, everybody will be the happier for blindly clinging to his passion and living as irrationally as possible. For reflection and worry make a desert of the soul; pleasure is never the outcome of clarity and wisdom, but invariably finds expression in intoxication, excess, frenzy, madness; a pinch of folly is needed to put savour into every genuine form of living, and the righteous man, the man of perspicacity, the man who is not the slave of his passions, is by no means to be considered a normal individual but an abnormality. "He only who has experienced folly in his own life is worthy the name of Man." Stultitia, therefore, sings her own praises, since she is the driving-force behind all human activity; with the eloquence of the Goddess of Persuasion she proclaims that the belauded virtues of this world, clarity of thought and correctness of vision, straightforwardness and honesty, have been invented merely to embitter the lives of men; and, since she is a learned dame, she quotes, for her better honour and glory, Sophocles' dictum: "Only in unreason is life a pleasant experience."

In proper academic style, Dame Stultitia develops her thesis point by point, and brings a crowd of witnesses to emphasize her arguments. Every estate, during the grand parade, is induced to display its own special delusion. She holds them all in review, the babbling rhetoricians, the hair-splitting lawyers, the philosophers each of whom imagines he can place the universe in his own particular sack, the proud of birth, the money-grubbers, the schoolmen and writers, the gamesters and warmongers, and, finally, those who are everlastingly slaves of their feelings, the lovers, who invariably imagine the object of their love to be the summit of all beauty and delight. A magnificent gallery of human folly is thus presented to us with Erasmus's inimitable knowledge of human nature, and such great writers of comedy as Molière and Ben Jonson merely needed to lift their materials from this amazing puppet-show in order, from

[83]

its delicate and elusive caricatures, to mould the forms of real men and women. No genus of human folly escapes detection, none is forgotten; the completeness of the picture acts as a safeguard for Erasmus—for who would venture to declare that he was singled out for condemnation when no one else was treated with less contempt than himself? For the first time Erasmus was able to show the universality of his culture, his intellectual force, his wit, his knowledge, his clear-sightedness, and his humour. His scepticism and the soaring superiority of his vision of the world burst into a hundred sparks and hues like a splendid rocket. A lofty brain finds fulfilment under sportive guise.

At bottom, however, this book was more than a joke to Erasmus, and he was able in the apparently small work to manifest his spirit more aptly than in any other because the *Laus Stultitiæ* was a kind of examination of conscience applied to Erasmus himself. He deceived himself neither as to persons nor things, knowing what underlay the seemingly most inexplicable of weaknesses, realizing to the full what it was that hindered him in his undertakings and prevented him from producing any genuinely creative work. He recognized that he was too rational and lacked passionate impulse, that his non-partisanship and his way of passing things by with averted eyes placed him outside the pale of the living. Reason is nothing but a regulative mechanism, it can never create out of its own energies; the really productive genius needs to have its illusions in order to give birth to that which is within it. Strangely lacking in this power of creating illusions for himself, Erasmus remained all his life a passionless man, cool-headed and fair-minded, never experiencing that greatest of joys, complete surrender, the lavishing of one's own self in holy ecstasy. In his *Moriæ* for the first and last time Erasmus shows that he knew and secretly fought against his inborn rationality, impartiality, sense of duty, moderation. And, since the artist works with a surer touch when he is dealing with something that he longs to possess and cannot, so in this instance the overrationalized author proved the best interpreter when it came to intoning a merry hymn in honour of folly and in the cleverest way to turn his nose up at the deification of pure wisdom.

Even so we must not allow ourselves to be deceived as to the motive lying behind the mask of comedy which the book presents to our outward gaze. This seemingly farcical *In Praise of Folly* was, beneath its carnival mask, one of the most dangerous books of its day, and that which appears to us as a witty firework is in reality a bomb whose explosion opened the road to the German Reformation. *Laus Stultitiæ* was one of the most effective pamphlets that ever was written. Alienated and embittered, the German pilgrims returned from Rome where they had seen popes and cardinals leading the same thriftless and immoral lives as the temporal princes of the Renaissance. Disenchanted and impatient, these genuinely religious men demanded a "reform of the Church from the head downwards and through all its limbs." But the pompous and showy popes paid no heed to entreaties, and the supplicants who spoke too loud or were too passionate in protestation were led gagged to the scaffold there to atone for their effrontery. In racy folk-songs and in sturdy anecdotes the bitterness felt at the misuse of relics as objects of commercial haggling, and at the sale of indulgences, found vent; clandestine leaflets bearing the image of the pope circulated freely among the population, and on some of these he was depicted as a huge blood-sucking spider. Erasmus publicly nailed the catalogue of curial crimes upon the wall of his epoch. Master of ambiguity as he was, he made use of his gift in magisterial manner, allowing his Stultitia to utter the dangerous and yet necessary strictures, and thus letting loose a determined assault upon the religious abuses of the day. Although such criticism was presented in farcical fashion, he who wields a verbal flail knows well enough what lies behind the words. "If the highest dignitaries, if the popes, those representatives of Christ on earth, were really to model their lives upon His, were to copy His poverty, were to bear His burdens, were to carry His cross, were to share His scorn for mundane things, who could be more worthy of compassion than they? How many treasures would the Holy Fathers have to forfeit if wisdom were suddenly to subdue their minds! Instead of untold riches, divine honours, the distribution of so many dignities and offices and dispensations, the pocketing of so many taxes and contributions, these people who had led such easy and enjoyable existences would have to spend their sleepless nights in prayer, would have to observe the fasts, would be expected to weep and to meditate and to pass their days in a thousand hardships." Then, suddenly, Dame Stultitia shakes off her fool's trappings and unambiguously demands an early reformation. "Since the whole of Christ's teaching rests upon meekness, patience, and contempt of the world, the meaning is obvious. Christ verily required that His representative should equip himself in the way He desired, and expected him, not merely to lay his shoes and his purse aside, but likewise his raiment, so that he should enter upon his apostolic duties stripped naked. He should take nothing with him but a sword, not the unholy weapon which serves the purposes of robbery and murder, but the sword of the spirit which pierces to the remotest recesses of the soul and at one blow destroys all passion, so that piety alone shall take up residence therein."

Imperceptibly the joke has turned into trenchant earnest. From beneath the fool's cap gleams the unerring and severe eyes of the greatest critic of his epoch. Foolishness spoke aloud what hundreds of thousands were secretly thinking. With greater strength, with more insistence, and with deeper knowledge and understanding, than in any other writing of that time, is the urgent need for a thorough reform within the Church brought home to the consciousness of Erasmus's contemporaries. Something always has to be destroyed if the new is to come into being. Before every spiritual revolution, the pioneer must lead the way—the critic, the enlightener, the creator, and the builder. The soil has to be ploughed before it will be ready to receive the seed.

Negation for negation's sake and unfruitful criticism were not in keeping with Erasmus's mental texture. When he showed up abuses, it was solely to demand that they be replaced by what seemed to him more jus-

tified and right; he never blamed in a spirit of arrogant
and carping censure. Nothing was more alien to this
man of tolerant character than a crass, iconoclastic assault upon the Catholic Church. As a humanist Erasmus
did not dream of a rebellion against the ecclesiastical
arm but of a "reflorescentia," a renascence of religion,
of a renewal of the Christian ideal by a return to its
Nazarene purity. Just as the Renaissance brought fresh
vigour into the arts and sciences by a study of the works
of classical antiquity, so did Erasmus hope that the
Church, bogged as it was in externals, might be trans-
figured by ridding it of contaminated sources and going
back to the teachings of the Gospels, by hearkening to
the very words of Christ, and "finding anew the real
Christ buried beneath the superimposed dogmas." Here,
again, we see Erasmus acting as pioneer, as leader in the
vanguard of the Reformation.

According to Erasmus, humanism can never be revolutionary, and, though he urged reform within the
Church and himself was the most important of those
who prepared the way, he could not, since he was of an
extremely pacific disposition, work for an open schism.
Erasmus never laid down the law, never violently re-
sented contradiction after the manner of a Luther, a
Zwingli, or a Calvin; he never dogmatized as to what

was right in the Church or what was wrong, which sacraments were acceptable and which were unacceptable, whether the Elements were substantial or insubstantial. He was content to insist that the true essence of Christian piety was not to be found in outward observance, but that the measure of a man's faith lay within him. It was not the worship of saints, or pilgrimages, or psalm-singing, or theological scholasticism with its sterile "Judaism," which made the Christian; but his spiritual trustworthiness, his human and Christianly way of living. "He alone does honour to the saints who imitates their virtues." It is not by collecting their dry bones, not by going on pilgrimages to their tombs and burning many candles to their memory, that a man proves his Christianity. Far more important than minute attention to ritual and prayer, to fasts and attendance at Mass, is that a Christian should order his life in the spirit of Jesus. "The quintessence of our religion is peace and unanimity." Here, as always, Erasmus's object is to raise the living up to the all-human rather than to petrify it in formulas. He wants to loosen Christianity from that which is purely ecclesiastical insofar as he can bring it into unison with the universally human. Everything which the peoples and religions have invested with ethical values he desired to see adopted into Christianity as an element of fruitfulness; and, though living in an epoch of narrow-minded and dogmatic fanaticism, this great humanist was able to deliver the splendid dictum: "Wherever you encounter truth, look upon it as Christianity." Therewith a bridge was built, linking up all times and all zones. He who, like Erasmus, sees wisdom and humaneness and morality everywhere, as forms of the higher humanity and as belonging to Christianity, cannot be, like the philosophers of old, banished into hell by monkish zealots ("holy Socrates," cried Erasmus once in a fit of enthusiasm); on the contrary, all that was noble and sublime in antiquity shall be roped into the religious fold, "as when the Jews in their flight from Egypt took with them their gold and their silver utensils to adorn the temple they would build." Nothing that has ever been of great moral meaning or of ethical significance to mankind should be, according to Erasmus's concept of religion, excluded from Christian doctrine, for among men there are neither specifically Christian nor specifically pagan truths; in all its forms, truth is divine. Erasmus, therefore, never spoke of a Christian theology, a tenet of faith, but of a "philosophia Christi," that is to say, a theory of right behaviour. Christianity is, for him, only another word for a lofty and humane morality.

[91]

In view of the architectonic strength of the Catholic exegesis and the ardent love displayed by the mystics, these fundamental ideas of Erasmus may appear rather jejune and commonplace, but they are human. In this matter as in the other fields of knowledge he approached, Erasmus may be said to have opened up vistas rather than to have plumbed depths. His *Enchiridion militis christiani* (a *Handbook for the Christian Fighter*), a work written at the request of a pious lady for the edification of her husband, became the theological textbook of the common people; and the Reformation, with its challenging and revolutionary demands, found in the book a field ready prepared for the sowing. But the mission of this solitary crier in the wilderness was not to open the battle; his vocation was to calm down at the eleventh hour the menacing conflict by proposing certain compromises and accommodations; for at that time in the Councils of the Church there were many disputes and much contention over insignificant details in the interpretation of dogma, and Erasmus dreamed of an ultimate synthesis of all forms of spiritual belief, of a "rinascimento" of Christianity, so that the world might for ever be freed from strife and counterstrife, and thereby that a belief in God might truly be made the religion of mankind.

The fact that Erasmus was able to express the same thought in many different forms shows how versatile he was. *In Praise of Folly* reveals abuses within the Catholic Church; the *Handbook for a Christian Fighter* presents us with the dream of a universally understandable ideal, a religion that would be more spiritual and more humane; simultaneously, by making fresh translations of the Gospels from Greek into Latin, he worked at the practical realization of his contention that Christianity must be freed from contaminated sources—thus paving the way for Luther's rendering of the Bible into the German vernacular.

Let us go back to the wellspring of true belief, let us seek truth there where she is still divinely pure and not sullied by dogma—these constituted Erasmus's demands upon the new humanistic theology; and with instinctive realization of the needs of the day he pointed to this work as that of the most decisive importance, fifteen years before Luther entered the arena. In 1504 he wrote: "I cannot find words to express the delight I feel when voyaging full sail across the Holy Scriptures, and how everything which keeps me away from them or merely interrupts my study of them annoys and disgusts me." The life of Christ, as recounted in the Gospels, must no longer be the privileged reading of monks and priests who happen to know Latin; the entire people must have part and lot in it; "the peasant shall read it while resting by the plough, and the spinner at his loom"; women must impart this core of Christianity to their children. But before Erasmus dared to carry out his idea of advocating that the Bible should be translated into the folk-speech, our man of learning realized that the Vulgate (the only translation that was tolerated by and approved of by the Church) was full of lamentable errors and obscure passages, and that from the philological point of view it was open to grave criticism. No earthly stain could be allowed to besmirch truth; so, firm in his conviction, he set himself to the formidable task of making a fresh Latin translation of the New Testament, with a critical commentary of his own in elucidation of the Vulgate's discrepancies and misinterpretations. This new Latin version was published by Frobenius at Basle in 1516. Its issue signified that a notable step forward had been made, for even in the theological faculty—the last to be touched by such an occurrence—the spirit of free investigation thus successfully penetrated. But it was typical of Erasmus that, even where he promoted a revolutionary change, he was so careful to maintain the outward forms of decorum that the staunchest blow never led to a collision. In order, at the very outset, to blunt the point of any theological attack, Erasmus dedicated this first free translation of Holy Writ to the ruler of the Church, to Pope Leo X, himself in sympathy with the humanist movement, who assured the author in a friendly breve: "We are greatly pleased." He even went on to praise the zeal with which the labour had been undertaken. As an individual, thanks to his conciliatory temperament, Erasmus always knew how to solve the conflict between ecclesiastical study and free investigation. Among his contemporaries this was far from being the case, and, consequently, the most furious enmities ensued. His genius as mediator, his art of bringing about a gentle agreement, triumphed likewise in this thorniest of spheres.

With these three books Erasmus conquered his epoch. He had spoken the enlightening word which solved the problems of his generation; and the calm, compassionate, humane way in which he coped with the most burning questions of the day brought him sympathy from all sides. Mankind is ever grateful to him who maintains it to be possible for progress to be made in a rational manner; and the new century looked with pleasure to the one man in Europe who was able to appreciate mental and spiritual things from the human point of view. Too long had ears been tired by the excited babble of monks, the quarrels of fanatics, by offensive gibes and lack of understanding on the part of the schoolmen. In Erasmus was to be found a heart that held the world in friendly affection; one who, in spite of grievous defects, believed in this world and wished to lead it into the realm of clarity. What invariably happens in such circumstances happened in Erasmus's case. When a man is determined to deal with the most ticklish problems of his day, there assemble around him those who share his views, and this body of faithful admirers increases the master's creative energies by the power of their serene expectation. All the forces, all the hopes, all the impatience of the period, were concentrated in this man who was expected to raise mankind to a higher ethical standard by means of the newly discovered sciences. "He or none," was on every lip. "He or none can snap the intolerable tension which we all of us feel in the air." Merely as a literary man, Erasmus's name became an incomparable power at the opening of the sixteenth century. He might, had he possessed a daring spirit, have utilized his position to perform some outstanding deed, some authoritative reforming act, that would have been of historical importance. But the world of action was not his world. Erasmus could clarify but not shape, he could prepare the ground but not garner the harvest. His name does not adorn the annals of the Reformation; another was to reap where he had sown.

GREATNESS AND
LIMITATIONS OF HUMANISM

BETWEEN the ages of forty to fifty, Erasmus attained to the zenith of his fame. For a hundred years or more Europe had known none greater. At the time when he flourished not one of his contemporaries, neither Dürer nor Raphael, Leonardo, Paracelsus, nor Michelangelo, enjoyed anything like the veneration which Erasmus received in the realm of the spirit; no other author of the day saw his works issued in such numerous editions; no moral or artistic respect granted elsewhere could be compared with that which accreted around him. To pronounce the name of Erasmus was, in the early decades of the sixteenth century, to call up the perfect image of the wise man, the optimum et maximum, the best that brain could conceive of and the most sublime—as Melanchthon writes in his Latin panegyric—the unsurpassed authority in matters concerning the scientific, the poetical, the mundane, and the spiritual achievements of his epoch. He was called "doctor universalis," and "prince of scientific learning," "father of study," "the protector of an honourable theology," the "light of the world," the "Pythius of the west," "vir incomparabilis et doctorum phœnix." No praise seemed too high to bestow on him. "Erasmus," wrote Mutian, "is suprahuman. He is divine, and should be venerated piously as though he were a creature come down to us from heaven." Camerarius, another humanist, declares: "Everyone who does not wish to remain a stranger in the realm of the Muses admires him, glorifies him, sings his praises. He who is capable of extracting a letter from Erasmus has already achieved fame and can celebrate a veritable triumph. But he who is allowed converse with Erasmus may count himself among the blessed that walk this earth."

In actual fact there was intense competition, among all who wished to cut a figure, for Erasmus's favours, though he had so short a while before been an unknown scholar who eked out a subsistence by incessant toil, writing dedications, giving lessons, and dispatching begging letters, who had to cringe to and flatter wealthy patrons in order to procure the wherewithal to live. Now the mighty wooed him—and it is invariably a glorious sight to witness earthly power and riches bending the knee before the predominance of the spiritual. Em-

perors and kings, princes and dukes, ministers and pro-
fessors, popes and prelates, were all of them rivals for
Erasmus's good will. Charles V, ruler of the New
World and the Old, offered him a seat in the
Aulic Council; Henry VIII wanted him to reside in
England; Ferdinand offered him a pension if only he
would consent to go to Vienna; Francis I promised him
a fine reception in Paris; the most tempting invitations
came from Holland, Brabant, Hungary, Poland, and
Portugal; five universities strove to obtain the honour
of placing him on the staff; three popes wrote him letters full of veneration. His room was cluttered with
tokens of esteem, free tributes from wealthy admirers.
There were golden goblets and silver table-services;
casks of finest wines were sent to him; rare and precious
books. Everything seemed to have set itself in motion
to tempt him to make the most of his celebrity. Erasmus, shrewd and sceptical as he was, accepted these gifts
and honours with courtesy. He allowed others to bestow presents upon him; he did not demur when his
name was praised and commended; on the contrary, he
enjoyed this good fortune with a feeling of ease and
comfort. But he was not to be bought. He accepted
service, but he gave none in return; always he remained
the incorruptible fighter for that inner freedom and un-

bribable integrity of the artist which he regarded as the necessary prerequisites for gaining an influence in the realm of morals. He realized that his strength lay in his independence; and, though it may seem a superfluous piece of foolishness on his part, he wanted his fame to precede him from court to court, instead of being fixed like a shining star above his own house. He no longer needed to travel in another's wake, for everyone journeyed to find him; Basle, because he dwelt there, became a residential city for the learned, the rallying-point for the whole intellectual world. No prince, no scholar, indeed no one who desired consideration, ever missed visiting the sage of Basle if chance took them near that town on their journeyings, for to have held converse with Erasmus came to be looked upon as a kind of cultural dubbing with knighthood, and a call at his house (as in the eighteenth century at Voltaire's and in the nineteenth at Goethe's) became one of the most obvious tokens of respect that could be paid to the symbolical carrier of the unseen power of the spirit. In order to possess a holograph signature of his name, nobles and men of learning would journey for days; a cardinal, nephew of the reigning pope, who had vainly asked Erasmus to his board, did not feel offended when the invitation was refused, nor did he consider it beneath his dignity to look Erasmus up in the fusty little room at Frobenius's printing-works. Every letter from Erasmus was folded in brocade by the recipient, to be displayed as a precious relic before the admiring gaze of friends; and a recommendation from the master acted like an open sesame at all doors. Never did a man (not even Voltaire and Goethe) enjoy so great a prestige in Europe, a prestige due entirely to his intellectual acquirements.

Looking back through the centuries, it is hard to understand why Erasmus should have held such sway over his time and generation, for neither his works nor his activities seem to warrant anything of the sort. He appears to us a sensible, humane, versatile, and multiform personality, an attractive and stimulating man; but in no wise one to sweep his fellows along in a mighty current and transform the aspect of the world. Yet in his own epoch Erasmus was more than a literary phenomenon; he was the symbolical expression of its secret spiritual longings. Eras about to be renovated project their ideal into a figure which shall manifest the soul of the age; for the Zeitgeist, if it is to grasp its own essence concretely, invariably chooses the type of man most suited to its purpose; and when this unique and chance-found individual outsoars his inborn capacities, it grows, in a sense, enthusiastic over its own enthusiasm. New feelings and new thoughts are understood only by a limited circle of the élite; the broad masses of the people are incapable of grasping them in their abstract form; they must have them rendered tangible to the senses and anthropomorphized. In the place of an idea, a man or an image or prototype is set up; and the faithful endeavour to model themselves upon this substitute presentment. The desires of the time found in Erasmus, for one brief historical hour, their fullest expression. The "uomo universale," the non-partisan, the rich in knowledge and learning, with his eyes looking freely into the future, became the ideal type of the rising generation. In venerating humanism, people paid homage to their own courage in the realm of thought and to their freshly formed aspirations. For the first time, intellectual authority was given precedence over inherited or transmitted authority; and that the change was brought about rapidly is shown by the fact that the wielders of authority submitted voluntarily to the new order of things. Symbolical of the day was it that Charles V, to the horror of his court, should stoop to pick up a paintbrush Titian's son had let fall; that the pope, rudely requested by Michelangelo to leave the Sistine chapel, meekly did so in order not to disturb the master; that princes and bishops began to collect books and pictures and manuscripts rather than weapons. Unconsciously they capitulated, recognizing that the power of creative thought had taken the reins of government, and that works of art were destined to outlive the works of war and of politics. Europe realized at last that her vocation and the whole meaning of her existence lay in the dominance of the mind and in the creation of a united civilization which should rally beneath its standard all the peoples of the West. Thus she would start a movement which would lead to the inauguration of a worldwide culture.

The spirit of the age, therefore, chose Erasmus as banner-bearer for the new way of thinking; and as "antibarbarus," as the fighter against all forms of backwardness and traditionalism, as harbinger of a higher, freer, more humane community of mankind, as the guide into the coming citizenship of the world, he took his place at the head of the marching column. We in our epoch feel that other figures were, perhaps, worthier of this position, such men as Leonardo and Paracelsus, for instance, who were more daring explorers, more sturdy fighters, more resembling the Faustian spirit, that personification of humanity, tempted and disquieted, but at length groping its way to the light. These were and are profounder types of "uomo universale," on a far more splendid scale than Erasmus could ever be. But the sixteenth century saw this not, and it was thanks to his clear (sometimes too piercing) understanding, his contentment at knowing the knowledgeable, his urbanity, that he owed his good fortune. And the instinct of the age acted rightly. The renewal which was fated to take place needed moderate reformers, not rabid revolutionaries; in Erasmus his contemporaries found the symbol to represent the incessant control exercised by reason. For a wonderful moment in time Europe lay dreaming the humanist dream of a united civilization—united in speech, united in religion, united in culture—with the age-long and disastrous contentions laid to rest. This unforgettable endeavour is inseparably connected with Erasmus of Rotterdam's name. His ideas, his wishes, his dreams, for a short space governed Europe; and it was his and is our misfortune that this pure longing for unity and peace among the peoples of the West only constituted an interlude in the bloody tragedy of our common fatherland.

Erasmus's imperium, which should have for the first time—oh, memorable hour!—encompassed all the lands and peoples and languages of Europe, was to have held gentle sway. It was to come into being not by the use of force, but by the aspiring and convincing energy of intellectual achievement, for the humanists detested anything which smacked of the mailed fist. Having been elected leader by acclamation, Erasmus exercised no dictatorial rights. Voluntary adhesion and inner freedom are the fundamental laws of this invisible kingdom. It was not through the intolerance hitherto exhibited by princes and religious fanatics that men of Erasmus's way of thinking hoped to lead mankind to adopt the humanistic and humane ideals they adumbrated. No; it was by lighting up the darkness that the roving beasts were to be lured into the bright realm, by gently convincing the ignorant and those who stood aside so that in the end they should of their own accord enter the circle of illumination. There is nothing imperialistic in humanism; in its domain there are neither foes nor thralls. He who refuses to belong to the select circle can remain outside if he prefers; no one compels him; he is not pressed forcibly to accept the new ideal. Every form of intolerance—and intolerance invariably implies misunderstanding—was alien to the doctrine of universal understanding. On the other hand, none were denied an entry into this spiritual guild. Anybody was eligible to become a humanist if he desired education and culture.

Men of any class, and women, too, nobles and priests, kings and merchants, the laity and the clergy, all had free access to this free community; none were asked whence they came and to what race or class they belonged, no inquiries were made to discover what was their native speech or the nation to which they owed fealty. Thus an unheard-of concept came to freshen European thought: the idea of supranationalism. Languages, which had hitherto formed an impenetrable wall between nation and nation, must no longer separate the peoples. A bridge would be built by means of a universal tongue, the Latin of the humanists. At the same time the concept of a fatherland for each nation would have to be proved untenable because it formed too narrow an ideal. It should be replaced by the European, the supranational ideal. "The entire world is one common fatherland," declared Erasmus in his *Querela pacis* (Complaint of Peace), and from this commanding position he looked down upon the senseless quarrels between the nations, the hatred between English, Germans, and French, to exclaim: "Why do such foolish names still exist to keep us sundered, since we are united in the name of Christ?" Disputes between Europeans seemed to the humanists to be the outcome of misunderstandings arising from too narrow-minded an outlook, too faulty an education; the duty of coming generations of Europeans would be to replace the vainglorious claims of petty princelings, of fanatical sectarians, and of national egoists by sympathetic cooperation, by emphasizing that which could lead to harmony, by raising the European spirit to preside over the national spirit, to change Christianity as a simple religious congregation into a universal and all-embracing Christliness, where love of mankind and a desire to serve meekly and devotedly should prevail. Erasmus, we see, aimed higher than merely achieving a cosmopolitan community. What he showed was a resolute will to create a new spiritual form of unity in the West. Before his day there had been men to promote the notion of a united Europe, the Roman Cæsars, for example, with their idea of the "pax Romana," Charlemagne, and, at a later date, Napoleon. But these autocrats worked with fire and sword, endeavoured to compel the nations to unite under the threat of violence and the fist of the conqueror, which weighed heavily on the weaker in order to bind them the tighter to the strong. The great difference between their idea and that of Erasmus was that to him European unity seemed to be a moral idea, utterly unselfish, a spiritual demand. With him began to be postulated the concept (which many are still advocating today) of a United States of Europe under the ægis of a common culture and a common civilization.

As a matter of course the first thing Erasmus claimed, as champion of this and of his other projects for mutual understanding, was the disappearance of force and in especial the disappearance of war, "the reef upon which so many good things are shipwrecked." He was the first man of letters to advocate pacifist ideals. During an era of perpetual warfare he penned no fewer than five works attacking war; in 1504, an appeal to Philip the Handsome, King of Castile; in 1514, another to the Bishop of Cambrai, in which we read, "as a Christian prince you might for Christ's sake do your best to secure peace"; in 1515, the renowned essay in the *Adagia* which bears the eternally true title, "Dulce bellum inexpertis" (only to those who have never experienced it does war seem beautiful); in 1516 he addressed young Charles V in strong terms in the course of his *Instructions for a Pious and Christianly Prince;* in 1517 appeared the *Querela pacis,* which was issued in every language and circulated widely among the masses, this "plaint of peace, rejected by all the nations and peoples of Europe, and driven forth and slain."

Even in those days, more than four hundred years

before our own time, Erasmus knew how little a straightforward lover of peace could count upon gratitude and acquiescence. "It comes to this, that if one ventures to open his mouth against war he is looked upon as not much better than a brute beast, as a fool, and as being unchristianly." But that did not prevent him, with ceaselessly renewed resoluteness, in an epoch when club-law prevailed, and the rulers were guilty of the most barbarous acts of violence, from raising his voice in condemnation of the bellicose attitude of the princes. He considered Cicero was right when he said that an "unjust peace was preferable to the most just of wars." A whole arsenal of arguments, to which we today might go in search of numberless weapons wherewith to attack war, was used by Erasmus, the lone fighter, against this plague. "When animals fall upon one another," he writes, "I can understand and forgive, for they act in ignorance. But men should not need to be told that war is of necessity unjustifiable since, as a rule, it harms not so much those who prepare for it and who carry it on; for usually the full burden of it falls upon innocent parties, upon the unhappy masses, who gain nothing either from victory or from defeat. The chief hurt accrues to those who have had nothing to do with it; and even when the luck of the fight is on our side this good fortune for one spells misfortune for the other." The idea of war cannot, therefore, find any modus vivendi with the idea of justice. Besides, he asks again, how could any war ever be justifiable? For Erasmus there existed no unique and absolute truth either in the theological realm or in the domain of philosophy. Truth is a thing of many facets; so, indeed, is justice. Therefore "a prince should in no matter be more cautious or slower to move than in deciding to make war. Nor should he be satisfied to be confident that right is on his side—for who is not prone to regard his own cause as just?" All that is right has two sides, all things are "tainted by bias, and coloured by the party spirit"; even when a man feels quite sure he is right, his right must not be defended by force and must never be achieved by force, for "war grows out of another war, and thus one war creates a second."

A man of intellect could never look upon a decision arrived at by a call to arms as the moral solution of a conflict. Erasmus expressly declares that in case of war breaking out the men of intelligence and learning in every land must not renounce their friendship towards one another. Their attitude must never be to strengthen the contrasts in outlook among the nations, the races, and the classes by means of a disintegrating partisanship; they must unflinchingly remain in the sphere of human-kindliness and justice. Their eternal duty is to fight against the "vicious, unchristian, and wild irrationality of war" by setting up the ideal of universal brotherhood and universal Christianity. His greatest reproach against the Church as the setter of moral standards is that she sacrificed the magnificent Augustinian idea of "universal peace in Christ" to aspirations for the conquest of worldly power. "Theologians and teachers of Christian living are not ashamed to remain causes of discord, incendiaries, and leaders of those movements which our Lord Jesus Christ hated most. . . . How is it that the bishop's crozier and the warrior's sword find themselves in one another's company, the mitre wedded to the helmet, the Gospels to the buckler? How can they deliver Christ's word and preach war from the same pulpit, and acclaim God and the devil in the same trumpet-blast?" The "ecclesiastical warrior" is a contradiction to God's holy word, for the term denies the sublimest message left by the Lord and Master when He said: "Peace be with you."

Erasmus becomes passionate whenever he raises his voice against war, hatred, narrow-mindedness; but this passion of indignation never troubles the clarity of his outlook upon the world. Idealist at heart, and sceptical through his rational way of thinking, Erasmus knew all the oppositions which would arise in the practical inauguration of that "universal peace in Christ," that autocracy of the humanistic reason. The man who, in his *Praise of Folly*, described every species of human illusion and human silliness, and the impossibility of teaching mankind to act better, did not belong to those idealistic dreamers who imagine that they can slay or even stun by the written word, by books, by sermons, and by tracts, the ever-present impulse towards violence which lies at the basis of human nature. He did not turn a blind eye to the fact that this lust for power and this joy in battle had been fomented in the veins of man since the days when he was still a cannibal, for hundreds and thousands of years; that they were dark survivals of the primal hate of one human animal for his fellow; and that hundreds, perhaps thousands, of years would be needed to educate him into a higher ethical standard, to raise him culturally, so that in the end he may leave the husks of his animal origins behind and become a member of a genuinely human race of men. Erasmus knew that elemental impulses were not to be conjured out of existence by gentle and elevating words; and he accepted the barbarism of the world as an incontrovertible fact, and as something that was inexpungeable. His own combats took place in other spheres; as a man of intellect he had to turn to men of his own kidney, not to the led and the misled, but to the leaders, the princes, priests, scholars, artists, to those whom he knew to be responsible for the unrest throughout Europe. His wide vision had long since informed him that the impulse to violence is not in itself a danger. Violence is scant of breath; it strikes out blindly and in a frenzy of rage; its will, however, is aimless; it takes short views, and after such mad attacks it sinks back upon itself powerless and limp. Even when violence proves contagious and morbidly infects whole groups, these loose gangs are speedily broken up, and they disperse as soon as the first wave of ardour is spent. Insurrections and rebellions have never been a genuine menace if they lack intellectual leadership. Only when the impulse to violence is inspired with an idea, or is made to serve an idea, do genuine "tumulti" occur. Then come the bloody and destructive revolutions, then the bands of ragamuffins get formed into a party hastening to obey the rallying-cry, then by organization is an army created, then does a dogma help to promote a movement. All the great and vehement conflicts that have arisen among men are more rightly described as the outcome of certain ideologies than as being due to the

violence and bloodthirstiness of the human animal; for
an idea may let loose the will to violence and drive it to
the attack. Fanaticism, the bastard begotten out of brain
and power, fancies itself dictator in the realm of
thought, so that only what it thinks is acceptable and
must be forced upon the whole universe; it thus splits
the human community into friends or foes, adherents
or opponents, heroes or criminals, believers or heretics;
since it recognizes no other system than its own and no
other truth than its own, it needs must resort to violence in order to curb and bridle the divine multiplicity
of phenomena and to bring everything under one yoke.
The forcible curtailment of mental latitude, of freedom
of opinions, every kind of inquisition and censorship,
of scaffold and stake—these evils were not brought into
the world by blind violence, but by rigidly staring
fanaticism, that genius of one-sidedness, that hereditary
enemy of universality, that captive of a single idea
which would shut the whole world up in a cage.

Therefore Erasmus the humanist, who his life long
was for ever pointing to what was universal in mankind
as being its loftiest and holiest possession, considered
that the intellectual could shoulder no heavier burden
of responsibility than when by a one-sided ideology he
furnished the ever-ready will of the masses with a pre-

text for deeds of violence, since thus he let loose primitive forces which far outran his intentions, and falsified his purposes however pure they might be. One man single-handed is capable of setting the hounds of passion into motion, but he is hardly ever capable of bringing them to heel again. He who breathes his word softly into sleeping fires must remember that he may fan these fires into destructive flames; he who arouses fanaticism by declaring that only one system of existence, of thought, and of belief is valid, must recognize that he may be promoting a fissure in the heart of humanity, and may bring about a spiritual or actual war against every other form of thought and being. Tyranny over thought amounts to a declaration of war against the mental freedom of mankind; and he who, like Erasmus, seeks a higher synthesis for all ideas, seeks a harmony that shall embrace the whole of humanity, must look upon every form of biased thinking, of unwillingness to understand, as an attack upon his own hope of bringing about a mutual agreement. The humanistically educated, the humanely minded man in the Erasmic sense, can never pledge himself unreservedly to any kind of ideology, for every idea strives in its own fashion to achieve hegemony; nor may he bind himself to any party, since every member of a party must of necessity be a partisan and see himself and feel himself and think of himself as adhering to that party. A man must at all costs guard his freedom of thought and of action, for in the absence of this freedom no justice is possible—and yet justice is the one idea which all mankind should share in common. To think in the Erasmic way is to think independently; to act in the Erasmic way is to work for mutual understanding. The Erasmic creed, which is equivalent to a belief in mankind, demands that the faithful shall never promote dissension, but unity; never encourage the partisanship of the biased, but, rather, shall broaden the bases of mutual understanding and shall initiate further understandings; the more fanatical the epoch, the more above party should the true humanist be, gazing upon human errors and perplexities with indulgence and compassion, acting as the incorruptible champion of intellectual freedom and of justice here below. Erasmus, therefore, considered that every idea had a right to existence, and none could make an exclusive claim to being correct; and he who had tried to understand even folly and to sing its praises could not feel antagonistic to any theory or thesis unless it endeavoured to do violence to others. A humanist, knowing so much, loves the world precisely because of its variegated manifestations, and its contrasts do not alarm him. Nothing is farther from his mind than to endeavour to abolish these contrasts after the manner of the fanatic and the system-monger who would like to see all values reduced to a common integer and every flower constrained to take one shape and one colour. This is the sign-manual of the humanist: never to look upon contrasts with an inimical eye; always to work with a view to bringing about unity even there where unity seems impossible to achieve; invariably to seek out what is human in everything. Since Erasmus endeavoured to conciliate within himself such apparently irreconcilable elements as Christianity and classical antiquity, free thought and theology, Renaissance and Reformation, he must have deemed it possible that at some future date mankind would be able to bring into a joyful harmony the kaleidoscopic variety of the human universe, and to transform its contradictions into a higher unity. This ultimate and universal understanding—spiritual understanding among all the peoples of Europe—is, as a matter of fact, the only sort of religious creed which the level-headed and rationalistic humanists were trying to establish; and they worked for this end as ardently as their contemporaries did for a belief in God, proclaiming their message of a belief in man, declaring that upon this idea the meaning, the goal, and the future of the world depended. Instead of one-sidedness there must be unanimity, and thereby an ever humaner world of men.

The humanists recognized one single road whereby to achieve this training towards humanism: Education. Erasmus, and those who shared his views, maintained that man would become more human by means of education through the printed book, for only the uneducated, only the unlettered, yielded irreflectively to his passions. An educated man, a civilized man—and herein we see the tragical failure in their reasoning—was no longer capable of resorting to gory violence, and when once the educated, cultivated, and civilized got the upper hand, chaos and brute force would inevitably disappear, and war and persecution of opinions would become anachronisms. In their overvaluation of the effects of civilization, the humanists failed to take account of the basic impulses and their untamable strength; in their facile optimism they overlooked the terrible and well-nigh insoluble problem of mass-hatred and the vast and passionate psychoses of mankind. Their view was too simple. For them there existed two layers, an upper and a lower: in the latter were to be found the uncivilized, rough, and passion-ridden masses; in the former lived the educated, the penetrating, the humanistic, the civilized. They fancied that the main business was accomplished when increasingly large portions of the lower layer were transferred satisfactorily to the upper. Just as in Europe an ever-increasing area of land is reclaimed and brought under the plough, whereas previously these lands had been the haunts of savage beasts, so also must it be with mankind. Gradually ignorance and roughness among the peoples of Europe would be extirpated, to be substituted by cleared and fruitful zones of humanity. Thus religious thought would be replaced by the ideal of an uninterrupted ascent of man. The concept of a progressive evolution (at a later date to be converted into a scientific method by Darwin) became under the ægis of the humanists an ethical ideal towards which the men of eighteenth- and nineteenth-century Europe strove. Even in our modern scheme Erasmic ideas play an important part. Nevertheless it would be erroneous to believe that humanistic culture and Erasmus's teaching were in any way democratic, and heralds of liberalism. Never for a moment did it enter Erasmus's head, never did it occur to his followers, that even the most insignificant rights should be granted to the folk, to the uneducated, to those who were still under age— for them, all the uneducated were "under age"; and, although in the abstract they loved the whole of man-kind, they were careful to eschew the company of the "vulgus profanum." If we examine their theories more closely, we shall see how the ancient arrogance of the nobly born has been replaced by another kind of arro-gance, by the pride of intellect which was to hold sway for three hundred years to come, and which held that only the man who was sure of his Latinity, who had passed through a university, had a right to judge what was right and what was wrong, what was moral and what was immoral. The humanists, in the name of rea-son, were just as determined to govern the world as were the princes in the name of authority and the Church in the name of Christ. They aimed at establish-ing an oligarchy, at inaugurating the dominion of an educated aristocracy; the best, the most cultured, οἱ ἄριστοι, were, in the Greek sense of the term, to take over the leadership of the "polis," the State. Thanks to their erudition, their clear and humanistic outlook, they felt that they had been singled out to act as medi-ators and leaders, to come to the rescue when the nations were waging war or quarrelling; nevertheless the im-provement they looked for was not to be brought about with the aid of the people at large, but over the heads of the masses. At bottom, humanism was, therefore, far from being a denial of the knightly order; it was a renewal of this order along intellectualist lines. The humanists hoped to conquer the world by means of the pen just as those others had conquered with the sword; and, like those others, all unconsciously, they created a social convention adapted to their needs, a convention which should set them apart from "barbarians," a convention with a kind of courtly ceremonial of its own. They raised themselves to a novel kind of nobility by translating their names into Latin or Greek equivalents so as to dissemble the fact of their plebeian origins: Schwarzerd became Melanchthon, Geisshüssler became Myconius, Oelschläger became Olearius, Kochhase became Chytræus, Dobnick became Cochläus, and so forth. They were careful to array themselves in black clothing with ample folds, to differentiate themselves even outwardly from their fellow-citizens. It was considered to be beneath their dignity to write a book or a letter in the mother tongue, just as a knight would have been scandalized had he been asked to march forth to battle on foot amid the troops instead of mounted on horseback. Each felt it incumbent upon him to deport himself with special seemliness when mixing with the herd of those who had not entered the sacred precincts; they avoided hasty speech, cultivated decorous and courtly ways, while their contemporaries were rude and boisterous in behaviour. In writing and in style, in speech and in conduct, these aristocrats of the intellect aimed at dignity of expression and of thought, so that in the humanists the last faint rays of the epoch of chivalry fluttered up anew after having been dimmed and laid to rest along with Emperor Maximilian's bones. This was an order of the mind whose insignium was the book in place of the cross. And, since the order of knighthood had had recourse to the uncouth violence of the cannon in order to maintain itself in power, this noble company of idealists would fight against the boorish impacts of the folk revolutionaries, Luther and Zwingli, with the no less effective weapon of beauty.

But such deliberate ignoring of the masses, such studied indifference towards the world of reality, rendered it impossible to give durability to the kingdom Erasmus hoped to establish, and sapped the vital energy from his ideas. The fundamental mistake of the humanists was that they wished to teach the people from the heights of their idealism, instead of going down among the masses and endeavouring to understand them and to learn from them. The academic idealists fancied that they were already in power, because their kingdom

spread over all lands, because in every country, at every
court, in the universities, monasteries, churches, everywhere, they had those that served the cause, they had
their envoys and legates, who proudly furthered the
progress of "eruditio" and "eloquentia" in the regions
where barbarism held sway. But, though their realm
was extensive, its roots did not go deep, it only influenced the most superficial layers, having but feeble re-
lations with reality. When enthusiastic messages reached
Erasmus almost daily from Poland, Bohemia, Hungary,
or Portugal, when emperors, kings, and popes sought
the philosopher's favour, how could he fail at times,
alone in the seclusion of his study, to give himself up to
the sweet delusion that the reign of reason had truly
begun? But behind this huge accumulation of Latin
epistles, he surely could not have been unaware of the
complete unresponsiveness of the masses? Surely he
could not have failed to hear the growing rumble of discontent arising from the depths? The "people" simply
did not exist so far as Erasmus was concerned; he considered the masses were unworthy the attention of a
refined and educated man, and it would be beneath his
dignity to woo the favours of "barbarians." Thus, humanism was for the happy few, not for the broad multitude; it was never anything better than a kingdom set

amid the clouds lighting up for one moment the whole
world, beautiful to contemplate, a pure picture painted
by a creative mind, looking down serenely from its unattainable heights upon the tenebrous world below.
Such an airy and artificial structure could make no stand
against a genuine storm; it was doomed to perish unre-
sistingly, and to fall into oblivion.

The tragic side of the humanistic movement, and, indeed, the cause of its decline, was that, though the
ideas which animated it were great, the men who were
its prophets proved inadequate. As always with arm-
chair philosophies, there was a tincture of the ludicrous
in these well-meaning efforts to better the world. Thoroughly earnest and honest, wearing their Latinized
names as if they were intellectual masks, the protago-
nists suffered from a dash of pedantry and vanity, so
that their loveliest theories were thinly coated with
these two far from attractive qualities. Erasmus's pygmy
followers are touching in their professorial and academic naïveté, having much in common with the excellent persons we meet in philanthropic and universal
improvement societies; theoretical idealists whose religion consists in a belief in the inevitability of human
progress, jejune dreamers constructing moral universes

while sitting at their desks and writing down thesis after thesis on the subject of everlasting peace—while in the world of reality one war follows upon the heels of another, and the very same popes, emperors, and kings who have enthusiastically acceded to these ideas of conciliation are simultaneously agreeing and running counter to one another and setting the world aflame. Should a new Ciceronian manuscript be discovered, the humanist clan would go wild with excitement, fancying the whole world would re-echo with the joyful tidings; every sympathetic pamphlet, be it never so unpretentious, roused their most ardent and passionate approval. But that which moved the man in the street, that which stirred the masses to the depths, all those things were ouside the pale; they did not even wish to know about them; and, since they continued shut up in their studies, the words they uttered lacked resonance, and could find no echo in the world of reality. It was owing to this disastrous seclusion, this absence of popularity, that the humanists were never able to produce a harvest out of their fecund ideas. The immense optimism which inspired the whole of their work could not grow into a healthy and fruitful plant and develop adequately, because among these theoretical pedagogues of the idea of human progress there was not one who

possessed the power of speaking to and being understood by the people. Thus a great and sacred thought
was doomed to rot away for several hundred years because the man did not exist who could convey it to the
masses.

And yet that historic hour, in which the sun of human trust shone with gentle effulgence down upon our
European earth, was a beautiful moment in time; and if
the delusion, that the peoples were already at peace and
united, was premature, still we must respect it, and
return grateful thanks that it ever existed. Men have
always been needed who would be bold enough to
believe that history is not a dull and monotonous repetition, the same game played over and over again under
different disguises, but have had an invincible confidence that moral progress is a reality, that mankind is
slowly climbing an invisible ladder to better things,
leaving behind its bestiality and attaining to godliness,
abandoning the use of brute force in favour of the rule
of a well-ordered mind, and that the highest, the final
rung where full understanding will be achieved is no
longer so very far aloft. The Renaissance and the humanistic movement combined to create a moment of
intense optimism throughout the western world. We
cannot do otherwise than love this epoch and admire its

wonderful illusion, since then, for the first time, mutual
confidence arose among the peoples of Europe, inspiring them with the idea that a higher, more knowledgeable, and wiser humanity would be created, outstrip-
ping in accomplishment even the civilizations of Greece
and Rome.

And at the outset it seemed as if these optimists were
right, for were not wonders and portents rife in those
days, marvels superseding all that had hitherto gone to
the making of the human story? Would it not seem that
Dürer and Leonardo were Zeuxis and Apelles reborn,
that Michelangelo was a new Phidias? Did not science
set order among the stars, and promulgate new laws for
the terrestrial globe? Gold, streaming from freshly discovered continents, created fabulous wealth, and this
wealth begot new arts. Gutenberg's invention made the
production of books so easy that the word of enlightenment could spread over the whole surface of the earth.
Ah, it could not be long now, cried Erasmus and his
disciples gleefully, before mankind, so lavishly endowed by the products of its own energies, would recognize its mission, its ethical purpose here below—to
live in fraternal concord, to act uprightly, and to ex-
tirpate every vestige of the bestiality handed down
from its animal ancestry. Ulrich von Hutten's cry

sounded like a trumpet call over the land: "It is a joy to be alive!" From the pinnacles of the Erasmic temple the citizens of a new world looked down upon a new Europe, and saw the sun rising on the horizon of the future, a light announcing that at long last, after a weary eternity of spiritual darkness, the day of universal peace was at hand.

But they were mistaken. The dawn was not the holy one they expected to shine over a gloomy earth; on the contrary, the light came from the brand which was to destroy with incendiary force the ideal world so confidently expected by the humanists. As the Germanic hordes of old swept down upon the world of classical Rome, so Luther, the fanatical man of action, backed by the irresistible force of a mass movement, sallied forth to swamp and to destroy this supranational dream. Before the humanists had properly set about inaugurating their schemes for world unity, the Reformation disrupted the intellectual harmony of Europe, destroyed the "ecclesia universalis," shattering the whole fancied structure as with the blows of a titan's hammer.

THE TITANIC ADVERSARY

SELDOM do those decisive forces, destiny and death, visit man without a warning. Before every visit they send an envoy bearing a message, so softly spoken that the words go unheeded by the recipient. Among the innumerable letters of sympathy and respect which Erasmus received and which for so many years covered his writing-table, there came one, under date December 11, 1516, from Spalatinus, secretary to the Elector of Saxony. In the course of a laudatory epistle interspersed with erudite comments, Spalatinus wrote that there was a young Augustinian friar in the town who felt a great respect for Erasmus's teaching but who differed from the master on the question of original sin. He was not a follower of Aristotle on the point that a man was righteous because he behaved righteously, but held that a man was righteous if he were given occasion to act righteously, "a person needs first a change of heart, then good works will ensue."

This letter is one of the minute stones which go to the composition of the vast mosaic known as the history of man. For the first time, though indirectly, Dr. Martin Luther—for the young Augustinian friar was none other than he—addressed the great master, and his initial protest already touched the central point around which the two paladins of the Reformation were in later years to fight as enemies. At the time when he received the letter Erasmus paid little heed to the impressions it conveyed. How should he, busy as he always was, wooed by the whole intellectual world, find time to dispute on theological matters with an obscure monk in the depths of Saxony? He passed the information by, little knowing that the hour had struck when his own life and that of the world at large were to take a new turn. So far he had stood alone, master of Europe and master of the new interpretation of the Gospels; now a mighty opponent had arisen. With gentle finger, hardly audible, Martin Luther tapped at the door of Erasmus's heart; his name had not yet been mentioned, but before long that name was to sound throughout the world as the heir and conqueror of Erasmus.

This first encounter between Luther and Erasmus took place in the abstract world; and never in subsequent years were they destined to meet in person. A kind of instinct made the two men avoid one another. And yet their names were frequently coupled, their portraits appeared side by side, they were both proclaimed the rescuers from the Roman yoke, and extolled as the first honest German reformers. History has deprived us of a magnificent dramatic episode, for it would truly have been a moving sight to see these two meet face to face in controversy. Seldom does destiny produce such fundamentally contrasted men as Erasmus and Luther, differing completely both as to character and as to physique. In flesh and blood, in norm and form, in mental capacity and in conduct of life, from the outward bodily manifestation to the finest of nerve-fibres they hailed from different and hostile races, so far as habit of body and mind were concerned. The conciliatory temperament as opposed to the fanatical, cosmopolitanism against nationalism, evolution versus revolution.

Let us consider the exterior differences. Luther, son of a miner and offspring of peasant stock, enjoying perfect health, palpitating with life, indeed shaken by the storm of his inborn energies, full of vitality and the grosser lusts such vitality entails—"I gorge like a Bohemian and gulp down my liquor like a German"—a swaggering, brimming, almost bursting piece of living matter, the embodiment of the momentum and fierceness of a whole nation assembled in one exuberant personality. When he raised his voice, it was as if an organ with all the stops out roared; every word was racy, pungent, spiced, like the rye bread, freshly baked, we find on the German peasant's table; all the elements may be sensed therein—the soil with its peculiar odour and its springs, with its manures and dungs; wild as a hurricane, disturbing, disquieting, the mighty voice raged over the German land. Luther's genius was to be found in his sensual vehemence rather than in his intellectual capacities. Just as he spoke, not dead Latin, but his live, native German—though with the addition of an amazing gift for vivid imagery—so also did he think in the same way as the folk to which he belonged, guiding the will of the masses to the highest potential of passion. He was redolent of the Teutonic peoples, of the protesting and rebellious German instinct pushing itself into the consciousness of the world; and, since the nation accepted his ideas, Luther became embodied in the history of that nation, giving back to its elements his own elemental and pristine vigour.

Having looked at this stout, thickset, hard-boned, full-blooded clod of clay called Luther, having contemplated the man whose low brow expressed the combative force of his will, reminding one of Michelangelo's Moses, having gazed our fill at this man of brawn, let us turn our eyes upon Erasmus, the man of intellect. Here we see skin as transparent as parchment, silky in texture, thin, the integument of a sensitive and cautious man. Their respective outward and physical aspects suffice to inform us that between such a couple no enduring friendship or understanding is possible. Sickly, trembling with cold in the shelter of his room, year in year out huddled in furs, perpetually below par (whereas Luther possessed an overplus of health), Erasmus always had too scant an allowance of everything with which his rival was abundantly supplied. Erasmus had to warm his sluggish and anæmic frame with good Burgundian wines, whereas Luther—contrasts in petty things are sometimes the most salient—needed copious draughts of "strong Wittenberg beer" in order to dull his alertness into refreshing slumber at night. When Luther spoke, it was as though the house were filled with the rumble of thunder, the church with a mighty wind, the earth with the uproar of an earthquake; at table, in the company of friends, he would bellow with laughter, and he was so fond of music—indeed, theology alone stood above this love—that he enjoyed lifting up his sonorous voice in song. Erasmus had a weak and gentle voice, resembling that of one suffering from consumption; he carefully trimmed and beautified his sentences, sharpening his words to the finest of points. Luther's speech rushed forth like a torrent, his quill moved with lightning speed "like a blind horse." Luther exhaled power; all who came into intimate contact with him, Melanchthon, Spalatinus, and even the Elector, were held in subservience to his domineering and virile personality. Erasmus exercised his power the more when he himself remained in the background; through books and letters, through the written word. He had nothing to thank his body for, wizened, poor, and sickly as it was; all the good he accomplished was due to his lofty, his wide, his all-embracing intellect.

Even the mental equipment of these two men had been fashioned in totally different forges. Unquestionably, Erasmus was a man of wider vision, of profounder knowledge; nothing was alien to his mind. Clear and colourless as the light of day, his abstract comprehension pierced to the heart of every mystery, illuminating every object it contemplated. Luther's horizon was far more circumscribed, but his penetration went even deeper; his world was narrower, inconceivably narrower, than was Erasmus's universe; but to all his thoughts, to all his convictions, he imparted some of the impetus of his own personality. He absorbed everything that came his way, and warmed it in the hot stream of his rich red blood; he fecundated every idea with his own vital energy, imbuing it with fanaticism; and what he had once recognized and accepted, he remained faithful to all his life. Every concept coalesced with his whole being, and to it he imparted the full magnitude of his dynamic strength. Dozens of times did Luther and Erasmus utter the self-same thoughts, but, whereas Erasmus exercised a titillating effect upon the minds of intellectuals, Luther's words, thanks to his torrential impetus, immediately became a popular slogan, a call to arms, a formative demand, racing forth into the world like animated firebrands to kindle the consciences of men. All that Erasmus sought was peace and tranquillity of soul; all that Luther sought was to create a tension and a convulsion of the emotions. Erasmus, the "scepticus," manifested his greatest strength when he spoke clearly, soberly, and collectedly; Luther, the "pater exstaticus," was at his best when fury and hatred leapt volcanically from his mouth.

Even when two such antagonistic temperaments work towards the same goal, they are bound to clash.

At the outset, both Erasmus and Luther desired the same thing; but their natures were so fundamentally different that they endeavoured to achieve the aim by utterly dissimilar methods. Enmity radiated round Luther. Of all the men of genius who have lived upon this earth, Luther was, perhaps, the most fanatical, the most unteachable, the most intractable, and the most quarrelsome. He could only tolerate those who were completely acquiescent with his views, so that he could make what use he would of them; those who said him nay served him as targets for his wrath, and provided him with material to grind to powder with his scorn. Erasmus, however, had made antifanaticism a veritable cult, and Luther's harsh, dictatorial tones cut him to the quick. Pummelling, foaming at the mouth, violent words, were to him—the citizen of the world whose highest aim was to conciliate all men of intelligence—actually and physically unbearable; and Luther's self-confidence (called by Luther himself "my confidence in God") seemed to Erasmus challenging in the extreme and almost blasphemous in a world full of error and illusion. For his part, Luther intensely disliked Erasmus's lukewarmness and indecision in matters of faith, his smooth-tongued pliability, his evasiveness, his lack of conviction which made it impossible to pin him

down to some definite and unambiguous pronouncement. The perfect phraseology of the scholar's artisti-
cally ornate eloquence was gall and wormwood to the
rougher and more downright rival. There was something deep in Luther's nature, and something equally
deep in Erasmus's nature; but the two depths were antagonistic. Foolish, indeed, is the notion that nothing
but externals and the hazards of life rendered it impossible for these two first apostles of the new interpretation of the Gospels (the "new evangelical teaching" as
it is usually styled in Germany) to join forces for the
common cause. The differences in colouring matter of
blood and tissue of brain made even such likenesses as
might have existed of so contrary a hue and shape that
the resemblance was lost. The twain were organically
different, and there existed no meeting-ground for their
mutual collaboration. This dissimilarity penetrated into
the brain and into the plexus of the instincts, through
the channels where the blood coursed, on into those
depths where conscious thought no longer governs.
They could deal gently with one another for reasons of
policy and out of consideration for the cause; like two
logs carried down on the current of a stream, they could
drift comfortably side by side; but at the first bend,
at the first loop in the river-bed, they were fated to ram

one another. The conflict thus arising was inescapable and proved to be of worldwide significance.

As was to be expected, the conqueror in this battle was Luther, not merely because he was the greater genius of the two, but also because he was more used to combat and was a merry fighter. Luther remained all his life of a pugnacious disposition, a born wrestler with God, with man, and with the devil. Warfare was for him not only a pleasure and an outlet for his energies, but likewise a means of salvation from himself. A skirmish, a quarrel, dissension, fisticuffs, were a kind of spiritual blood-letting for Luther; and it was only when he came to blows, only when a tussle was in full swing, that he felt himself to be the man he was and filling to the full his manly measure. With passionate delight he hurled himself into the fray, whether the cause happened to be a righteous one or an unrighteous one. "An almost deathly shudder runs down my back," writes Bucer, Martin Luther's friend, "when I recall the fury that boils up within the man as soon as he comes face to face with an opponent." It is undeniable that Luther fought like one possessed when he went forth to battle, fought with his whole body, fiercely, with bloodshot eyes, and foam on his lips; and his "furor teutonicus" seemed to act as a purge on the feverish poisons within him. In actual fact, it was only when striking out in a blind frenzy, releasing his anger, that he felt light-hearted. "My whole bloodstream is refreshed, my 'ingenium' becomes clarified, and temptation is laid to rest." In the arena the erudite doctor theologiæ was instantly transformed into a soldier. "As soon as I arrive, I deal blows with my cudgel." A mad uncouthness, a berserker rage, seized upon him, he laid about him with any weapon that came handy, with the shining sword of dialectic or with a pitchfork heaped with dung and boorishness; any impediment to his onslaught he ruthlessly flung aside; and he did not recoil from untruthfulness and calumny if it was a question of laying an adversary low. "If you want to better humanity and reform the Church, you cannot afford to fight shy of a good, thumping lie." Chivalry was alien to this peasant fighter. Even when a foe had got his gruelling, Luther could not treat him with generosity or compassion; he continued to drub him in blind rage as the poor thing lay defenceless on the ground. Not for him the adage dear to the English: "Don't hit a man when he is down!" He rejoiced when he learned that Thomas Münzer with ten thousand peasants had been done to death, and boasted that "their blood is on my head"; he shouted with glee when "that swine" Zwingli, together with Karlstadt and all those who opposed his ideas, perished miserably; never once did this hot and mighty hater put in a word to save an enemy condemned to death. From the pulpit his voice rang forth carrying men along in a stream of enthusiasm; in the home he was a cheerful and friendly father and housemaster; as an artist in words he gave expression to the magnitude of his cultural attainments; but so soon as battle was joined, Luther was transformed, becoming a werewolf raging with uncouth and unjustifiable scorn and fury. Out of the dire necessity of his nature he was again and again forced into combat; for, not only did he enjoy this, considering it to be the jolliest thing in life, but he looked upon a fight as, morally, the fairest and justest form of activity. "A man, and especially a Christian, must be a warrior," he said proudly as he gazed at himself in a mirror; and in a letter written in 1541 he raised this concept into the heavens with the strange remark: "Certain is it that God is a sturdy fighter."

Erasmus, as Christian and as humanist, could not conceive of a combative Christ or a fighting God. Hatred and the desire for revenge seemed to him, the aristocrat of culture, a lapse into the plebeian and the barbaric. Any kind of tumult or rioting, every violent discussion, nauseated him. As a born conciliator and mediator, he was as loath to put up a fight as Luther was delighted to enter the battle-ground. Characteristically enough, he once observed in regard to this pusillanimity of his: "If ever I were given a fine estate in the country but had to go through the law courts to enter into possession, I would prefer to renounce the gift." Erasmus certainly loved a discussion among equals, but only as the nobles of old were fain to splinter a lance with their peers; it had to be fine and fair jousting, witty, wise, supple, with weapons steeled in the classical fires and suited to the forum of humanistic culture. To strike a few sparks, to succeed in some fresh ruse, to unhorse your opponent by a gibe at his faulty Latin—such intellectual sport was by no means foreign to Erasmus; but he was never able to understand Luther's exultation in the tourney, never able to see what pleasure the Wittenberg gladiator could take in trampling on his fallen foe; never having in his manifold writings passed beyond the borders of polite expression and decorum, he could not fathom why Luther should give himself up to such "bloodthirsty" hatred in his disputations with antagonists. Erasmus was not only a born pacifist, but his lack of positive conviction in his chosen articles of faith stressed the fact that he was no fighter; objective minds are usually lacking in self-confidence. Doubt comes only too easily to ruffle their clear surfaces, men of that calibre are given to reflecting upon the arguments set before them. But to allow an opponent the chance of uttering a word signifies that you have given elbow-room, and the only adequate way of fighting is to go at it madly, to draw down the ear-caps of defiance in order not to hear any voice but your own, and to protect your demoniac rage by putting on a hard and scaly skin. To the ecstatic monk, Martin Luther, every person who contradicted him was an emissary from hell, an enemy of Christ, a vile creature, vermin that it was incumbent to destroy; whereas, with Erasmus, even the wildest excess indulged in by an opponent was a matter for pity and regret. Zwingli gave us an admirable picture of the characterological contrasts between these two rivals, comparing Luther to Ajax and Erasmus to Odysseus: Ajax-Luther, typifying the courageous man of war, Odysseus-Erasmus, as he who enters the field of battle at the call of chance, returning home unruffled to the peaceful island of Ithaca, the isle of contemplation, returning from the realm of action to the realm of the spirit, where temporal victories or defeats appear to be void and empty things when likened to the inconquerable and stable actuality of Platonic ideas.

Erasmus knew very well that he was not made for war. If, against the dictates of his own heart, he did enter the fray, he invariably capitulated; for it is ever thus. When an artist or a man of learning exceeds his own limitations and gets in the way of the men of action, the men of might, the men who live for the passing hour, the former's power is reduced. An intellectual cannot afford to take sides, his realm is the realm of equable justice; he must stand above the heat and fury of the contest.

Erasmus failed to hear the first gentle warnings concerning Luther. Soon he was compelled to attend, and the new name became engraven in his heart. The sledge-hammer blows with which the Augustinian monk nailed his ninety-five theses to the church-door at Wittenberg echoed throughout the land. "As if the angels themselves were acting as messengers," so did the sheets, still damp from the press, pass swiftly from hand to hand. Betwixt night and morning the name of Martin Luther took its place side by side with that of Erasmus in the mind of the whole German nation, the two representing for their compatriots the most intrepid champions of a free Christian theology. With the instinct of genius, the future protagonist of the people's rights hit upon the very point which was proving a peculiarly sore one to the German folk, and one whereby Rome made its yoke most oppressively felt: the sale of indulgences. There is nothing a nation objects to more keenly than having to pay tribute to a foreign power; in this case the Church traded upon a fundamental anxiety present in every religious mind, employing agents to sell papal indulgences on commission, engaging professional salesmen to convert the papal tickets into coin of the realm. That the hard-earned money of peasants and artisans should travel across the frontiers to fill the chests of the Roman curia had long rankled, and a mute indignation was prevalent everywhere. Luther, by his challenge, merely set light to the conflagration. The materials for a bonfire were already piled. Nothing shows more clearly that it is not reproof of a wrong, but the form the reproof takes, which is of historical importance. Erasmus, too, and many a humanist, had expostulated against these sales, against the whole idea of buying yourself free from purgatorial fires, and had emptied the vials of their scorn upon the absurd business. But derision and laughter exist only as negative forces, they are not capable of assembling energies for a creative impact. Luther, however, was of a dramatic temperament, I feel inclined even to say that his was the only genuinely dramatic nature in the whole of German history. This gave him the wherewithal to make drastic use of primitive and unteachable instincts, to render his thoughts comprehensible to everyone; from the first he possessed that which has always proved irresistibly attractive to the masses, the eloquent and plastic gestures of a born orator, the happy phrase which is easily turned into a slogan. When he curtly and clearly declared in his theses, "the pope cannot forgive sin," or "the pope can mitigate no penance except that which he himself has imposed," these words were lightning-flashes of illumination, like thunder they roared down into the consciences of men, making the basilica of St. Peter in Rome sway beneath the storm. Whereas Erasmus and his disciples, by their mockery and their criticism, aroused the attention of the learned without ever reaching so much as the periphery of the masses, Luther at one stroke penetrated to the depths of folk-feeling and folk-passion. Within two years of the publication of his theses, Luther had become a symbol typifying the German nation, the tribune denouncing all that spelled Rome, the promulgator of the wishes and demands of the people, the concentrated force of every opposition.

A contemporary as keen-eared and as clear-sighted as Erasmus must indubitably have heard very soon of Luther's action. It should have gladdened his heart to know that an ally of such calibre was at hand, and that he possessed a comrade who would fight shoulder to shoulder for free theology. At first, no word of censure passed Erasmus's lips. "The good must love Luther for his courage," and "Luther, so far, has certainly been of use to the world"—it was in these kindly noncommittal phrases, when in conversation with his humanistic friends, that he referred to Luther's apparition. Still, even at the start, Erasmus gave cautious expression to a slight scruple when he said: "Luther has criticized many abuses admirably," adding with a sigh: "If only he could have done so with more moderation." A sensitive man like Erasmus always perceives the danger of an overfervid temperament such as Luther's. He sent out urgent warnings, begging his rival to use somewhat greater discretion. "It seems to me that gentleness achieves more than turbulence. It was through gentleness that Christ conquered the world." Thus, Erasmus was not disquieted by the actual words Luther spoke, nor by the phrasing of the theses, but by the tone of the ex-Augustinian's discourses, the demagogic and fanatical form which pervaded the man's every action. Such thorny problems in theology are, maintained Erasmus, best discussed quietly and among persons of

trained intelligence; the "profanum vulgus" should be
held aloof by the use of the academic language—Latin.
Theology could not be argued about from the house-
tops and at every street-corner; shopkeepers and cob-
blers were not fitted to discuss subtle things they were
unable to understand. Every discussion held in public
was considered by the humanists to lower the level of
that same discussion, and inevitably to incur the risk of
degenerating into "tumultus," into a riot of popular excitement. Propaganda and agitational work were proper
and right, and Erasmus believed in their unflagging
power. It seemed to him that once an idea had been
launched upon the world by means of the written or
spoken word, its significance and purport should be
spread abroad along spiritual and intellectual paths; that
it did not need the approbation of the masses or the for-
mation of a party to render it truer and more actual. A
man of intellect had, such was Erasmus's conviction,
nothing other to do in this world than to determine and
elucidate truths; his not to march forth and fight for
these truths. It was not envy, as many have maintained,
but a feeling of genuine and honest anxiety, a sense of
intellectually aristocratic responsibility, which led Erasmus to demur, for he saw that the storm of words uttered by Luther would be followed by a dust-cloud

raised by the excited masses who would follow in the great leader's wake. "If only he could be more moderate," Erasmus complained over and over again, feeling in his bones with the prophetic instinct of the wise that his sublimely spiritual realm of "bonæ litteræ," the sciences and the humanistic movement, would never be able to stand up against such a tempest. Even so, Luther and Erasmus never directly corresponded with one another, always did these two most noted masters of the German Reformation maintain an impenetrable silence one towards the other. Little by little so obstinate a silence became manifest to everyone. Erasmus, the cautious, had no inclination to make personal acquaintance with this unaccountable fellow; and, as for Luther, the deeper his own convictions led him into the fray, the more he looked askance at his sceptical contemporary. "Human affairs mean more to him than divine things," Luther wrote of Erasmus—showing with a masterly stroke of the pen the distance that lay between them: for Luther, the religious was the thing of greatest importance on earth; for Erasmus it was the human.

But by this time Luther stood no longer alone. Without any active desire on his part, perhaps without even realizing what his initial efforts were leading to, he had become the exponent of our many-sided terrestrial interests, the battering-ram of German nationalist aspirations, and an important piece on the political chessboard in the game between the Pope and the Emperor, and the numerous German princes. His demands had been made with a view to the spiritual reform of the Church. Now, after his first success, a number of persons whose outlooks were utterly foreign to his purpose and whose ideas were far from being evangelical in complexion, gathered round Luther to pick up any advantages that might accrue and thus to exploit the great man for their own purposes. Gradually, a nucleus formed itself around the master, handy material for a future party, preparing the way for the advent of a new religious system. But long before the massed troops of Protestantism were assembled, a general staff had been formed, among whom were Melanchthon, Spalatinus, priests, aristocrats, and scholars. Ambassadors from other lands looked on inquisitively to see what would be the upshot of these activities in electoral Saxony, wondering whether this ruthless fellow might not be fashioned into a wedge to be hammered into the structure of the empire. A finely meshed web of political diplomacy was slowly being woven round Luther's purely ethical and moral claims. His intimate circle of adherents was on

the look-out for allies, and Melanchthon, who knew
very well what an uproar the publication of Luther's
An Address to the Nobility of the German Nation
would create, pressed the demand that so noteworthy
an authority as Erasmus, celebrated for his unpartisan-
ship throughout the scholarly world, should be won
over to the evangelical cause. In the end Luther yielded,
and on March 28, 1519, he for the first time addressed
himself personally to Erasmus.

Flattery and an excess of polite diction were such
habitual phenomena among humanistic correspondents
that we need not be surprised at the exaggerated self-
abasement expressed in the opening sentences of this
celebrated letter. "What man alive has not his mind full
of thoughts concerning Erasmus? Whom has he not
taught, whom does he not govern?" And the writer
went on to describe himself as a dull, fat fellow with
unwashed hands, who had not yet learned how to compose a letter suitable for perusal by so great a scholar as
Erasmus. But since he had been told that his name was
not wholly unknown to Erasmus—owing probably to
his (Luther's) insignificant remarks anent indulgences—
persistent silence between the two seemed no longer
possible if malevolent tongues were not to be set wag-
ging. "I would beseech you therefore, most benevolent

of men, that you deign to notice this poor little brother in Christ, who is certainly unworthy your attention since his ignorance keeps him buried away in a dark corner, and who can claim no right to live under the same heaven and the same sun as you. . . ." The whole letter was written in order to lead up to this sentence. It contains all that Luther hoped to gain from Erasmus, which was a letter of acquiescence, a word of friendly approval of the writer's teaching, a line which would be (as we say nowadays) of "publicity value." The moment was a dark one for Luther and decisive for his whole future; he had declared war against the powers that be; the bull Exurge Domine was lying at Rome ready to be launched upon him at any time. To have Erasmus at his side as moral supporter would be a significant gain, and might, indeed, be a decisive factor in the victorious outcome of the Lutheran cause—for Erasmus's name was associated in all men's minds with complete incorruptibility. A non-party man is invariably the most important asset for the party man, and the finest standard round which to rally sympathizers.

But Erasmus was always loath to shoulder responsibility, and felt disinclined to stand security for an incalculable debt. If he agreed with Luther in this instance, he would pledge himself to acquiesce in everything the hothead should set down in future books and pamphlets and attacks, would consent to everything this immoderate and uncurbable creature might wish to promulgate, an author whose "violent and inciting manner of writing" was painfully irritating to the preacher of concord and unanimity. Besides, what was Luther's cause? The promise to take a person's part, to rally to his side, would mean the sacrifice of one's own moral freedom, to accept certain demands whose consequences none could possibly foresee. Erasmus would never consent to having his liberty of action or of thought curtailed. Maybe, too, the scholar's keen ecclesiastical sense of smell had nosed out a slightly heretical scent in Luther's writings. To compromise himself unnecessarily was not Erasmus's way if he could help it; his cautious disposition had deprived him of the power to give himself whole-heartedly to any cause.

He was careful, therefore, when replying, to give his correspondent neither a plain Yes nor a definite No, but to build a redoubt, from behind which he could peer to right and to left, hemming and hawing, and informing Luther that he had not read the latter's writings carefully enough to give an opinion. In actual fact, wrote Erasmus, since he had been ordained a priest of the Roman Catholic dispensation, it was strictly forbidden him to read any work antagonistic to the Church. Thus he furnished himself with a clever excuse for evading the issue. He thanked his "brother in Christ," telling him of the immense excitement Luther's books had raised in Louvain and how hatefully those in disagreement were behaving—by this means Erasmus was able to hint in which direction his own sympathies lay. It is a masterly piece of composition, and, reading it today, one realizes that this passionately independent man was determined to give no clear and definite word which would provide his correspondent with a pretext for pinning him down and making any further claim upon him. Referring to Luther's *Commentary on the Psalms*, he declares: "I have only fluttered the pages" (degustavi), i.e., he had not read this work either. He hoped that it would prove of great utility—again an evasive wish and conveying no definite judgment. Then, in order to widen the distance between Luther and himself, Erasmus made fun of the rumour that he was one of the committee engaged upon composing an indictment against Luther's works; the notion was ludicrous and malevolent. At the close, however, Erasmus became clear-spoken. Curtly and without circumlocution he declared that he had no wish to be drawn into the discussion. "So far as may be, I wish to keep neutral (integrum) in order to continue to do my share in promoting the renascent sciences; and I believe that a shrewdly manipulated reticence will achieve more than impetuous interference." Urgently he begged Luther to show more moderation, winding up with the pious and noncommittal hope that Christ might endow the Augustinian from day to day with an increasing measure of His divine spirit.

Therewith Erasmus took his stand, the same he had taken during the Reuchlin affair when he proclaimed: "I am not a member of Reuchlin's party; indeed I refuse to have anything to do with party. I am a Christian, and recognize the existence of fellow-Christians. But I refuse to be either a Reuchliner or an Erasmian." He was determined not to budge an inch farther than he wished to go. He was of an anxious turn of mind; but anxiety sharpens the faculty of observation so that it often brings sudden and clairvoyant prevision of coming events. Possessing greater clarity of vision than any of the other humanists who were then acclaiming Luther as a saviour, Erasmus was quick to recognize in Luther's aggressive and unqualified methods the omen of "tumultus"; he saw that what was likely to take place was a revolution rather than a reformation, and he would on no account enter these dangerous paths. "How should I be able to help Luther by merely turning myself into a companion in danger? By so doing I should lead two men to their deaths instead of one. . . . He has said a few excellent things, he has given good warning. How I wish he had not interfered with the working of these pre-eminent achievements by falling into his insufferable errors. . . . But even if he had said what he had to say in polite and decorous language, I would not have deliberately placed my head in danger for truth's sake. Not everyone has the strength for martyrdom; and I am afraid I must sadly admit that, were a tumult to occur, I should act the part of Peter. I obey the decrees of popes and and princes when I feel that they are just, and I tolerate their bad laws because such an attitude is the safer. A similar attitude, I firmly believe, might with advantage be adopted by all those who feel that resistance would prove hopeless." It was due no less to his spiritual faint-heartedness than to his unshakable desire for independence that Erasmus took the resolution never to fight for any cause in common with others, Luther's not excepted. Luther must go his own way, and Erasmus must be allowed to go his; they therefore came to an agreement that neither should enter into open conflict with the other. The offer of an alliance having been rejected, they concluded a pact of mutual tolerance. Luther's role was to furnish the dramatic element, and Erasmus hoped—vainly as it proved! —to be permitted to play the part of onlooker, of "spectator." "If God, as may be surmised by the magnificent swing with which Luther's cause has gone forward, wishes that matters should run this course and needs a rough-handed surgeon like Luther to heal the sores of a degenerate epoch, it is not for me to question His wisdom."

Nevertheless, in times of war it is a harder task to keep out of the fray and to preserve a perfect mental poise than to take sides, and much to his vexation Erasmus found himself between the cross-fires of parties each of which wanted to claim him as adherent. Erasmus started the criticism which was launched against the Church, but Luther transformed criticism into an active onslaught upon the papacy, so that a motto coined by Catholic theologians became current even during Erasmus's lifetime: "Erasmus laid the egg and Luther hatched it." Willy-nilly, Erasmus was the precursor, making the path smooth for Luther's valiant deeds: "Ubi Erasmus innuit, illic Luther irruit." Where Erasmus was content cautiously to set the door ajar, Luther turbulently flung it wide. Erasmus himself had to admit, when writing to Zwingli: "Everything which

Luther is demanding I, too, have taught, but not so vociferously and without going to such extremes of language." Method alone divided these two men. They both made the same diagnosis: that the Church was in mortal peril of a hopeless inward rot while preserving the outward semblance of stability. But whereas Erasmus proposed gradual amelioration, a careful and progressive course of blood-cleansing by means of the salt injections of reason and mockery, Luther went at the patient with the bistoury and made a bold incision. Such a dangerous intervention very naturally left Erasmus breathless with alarm, especially since he had a horror of the sight of blood. He strongly opposed such drastic measures. "I am resolved rather to let them pull me to pieces limb by limb than to give my sanction to dissensions, especially where questions of religious belief are concerned. I know that many of Luther's followers act upon the saying, 'I come not to send peace, but a sword.' Though I see much in the Church that it might advantage religion to change, I am averse to any action which might lead to commotion and uproar." With determination worthy of a Tolstoy he refused to admit that an appeal to force was legitimate, declaring himself ready to continue suffering an abuse rather than to raise a "tumultus" by resorting to violence and bloodshed.

While his fellow-humanists, more short-sighted and op-
timistic than he, were welcoming Luther's deed as an
act of liberation for the Church and as the redemption
of Germany, Erasmus realized that it would mean the
disruption of the "ecclesia universalis," the creation of a
national church in lieu of a worldwide church, and the
severance of Germany from participation in the unity
of the West. His heart told him what he could hardly
have understood through reason alone, that such a severance of Germany and the other Teutonic countries
from the papal dominion could not be brought about
except through one of the bloodiest and most homicidal
conflicts the world had ever known. Since war spelled
for him a step backward in the progress of civilization,
a lapse into the barbarism of epochs long since outlived,
he put all his strength into the scale to prevent this ultimate catastrophe from overtaking Christianity. With
this resolve firmly established in his mind, Erasmus took
on a duty of historical significance, a duty which, it
must be confessed, exceeded his capacity: alone, amid
the multitudinous exacerbations of the day, he set himself the task of incorporating the spirit of unclouded
reason, to defend the unity of Europe, the unity of
the Church, the unity of mankind, and the world-
citizenship of humanity with the pen as his only weapon,

and thus to protect all he loved against decay and anni-
hilation.

Erasmus began his self-appointed mission by endeavouring to put a curb upon Luther. Through the intermediation of mutual friends he besought Luther to be
less incendiary in his writings, to teach the Gospel in
less "unevangelical" terms. "I wish Luther could make
up his mind to forgo quarrelling for a while, and could
deal with evangelical reform without mixing it with
other things. He would thus achieve even greater success." Above all, it was unwise to discuss every question
in public; especially, the demand for reforms within
the Church was not a suitable subject to shout about
from the house-tops to a contentious and brawling mob.
The diplomat in Erasmus led him to belaud that virtue
of the man of intellect, the sublime art of silence at the
proper season in contradistinction to the agitator's art
of oratory. "We must not invariably tell the whole
truth. Much depends upon how truth is made known."

The mere suggestion that truth might be withheld
for mundane advantages, were it but for a moment, was,
it need hardly be said, utterly incomprehensible to Luther. For him it seemed the highest duty that every iota,
every syllable, of the truth a man's heart and mind had

once accepted must be confessed, must be shouted aloud, no matter if a war, a tumult, or the falling-down of the firmament should arise therefrom. The art of keeping silence was not to be acquired by a Luther, nor did Martin Luther wish to learn it. During the four years since his theses were published, he had learned a new and mighty speech; immeasurable powers, indeed the full tide of popular resentment, had come to his support; the Germans' awareness of themselves as a nation, their revolutionary eagerness to be in arms against foreigners and the empire, their hatred of priests and of outsiders, the sullen social and religious fervour which since the peasant revolts, with their ominous watchword "Bundschuh, Bundschuh, Bundschuh," had been fermenting among the countryfolk—all this had been roused to activity by Luther's hammer-blows upon the church-door at Wittenberg. Each estate, princes and peasants and burghers alike, felt that their personal claims and their rights as citizens had been hallowed by the Gospels. The entire nation, hitherto rent by local squabbles, put its passionate trust in Luther because in him it saw a man of courage and of action. Now, whenever the national cause and social demands are mixed in the same crucible with religious ecstasy, an earthquake is engendered, shaking the world to its foundations; and should, moreover (as was the case with Luther), a man appear at the appropriate hour whom the multitude can recognize as the embodiment of their own unconscious will, that man will become the vehicle of magical powers. He who, at a word, is chosen to wield the mighty energies of a nation is often tempted to look upon himself as a messenger from the godhead. Thus after incalculable years a man arose in Germany speaking with the tongue of the prophets. "God has commanded me to teach and judge here in Germany as did the apostles and evangelists of old." From God's very self the mission had been received to cleanse the Church of its abuses and to deliver the German peoples out of the hands of "Antichrist," of the pope, "that popinjayed and tangible devil"—to deliver by means of the word and, if that means failed, then by way of the sword and fire and blood.

To preach caution and discretion to ears that are deafened by the joyous uproar of a nation and into which God has whispered His divine injunctions is obviously to waste one's breath. Soon Luther came to pay no heed whatsoever to what Erasmus wrote or thought; the younger man no longer needed the older. With iron strides, and inexorably, Luther marched forward along the path which destiny had traced for him.

With the same energy he had expended in warning
Luther, Erasmus now turned to admonish the other side
—pope, bishops, princes, and those set in authority. In
this camp, too, he beheld his ancient enemy at work,
beheld fanaticism rampant, a fanaticism utterly incapable of recognizing wherein it erred. He suggested that
the papal ban had, perhaps, been premature; that Luther
was a thoroughly honest and upright man, whose tenor
of life was praised by all and sundry. True, Luther had
entertained doubts concerning the validity of indulgences, but others before him had raised objections to
them. "Not every error need be heretical," cried this
born mediator, thereby vindicating Luther's attitude.
Even though writing about his bitterest foe, Erasmus
could still declare that "Luther acted precipitately,
maybe, but certainly not with evil intent." In such circumstances it was not imperative to clamour immediately for the stake, and not every suspect could be right-
fully accused of heresy. Would not the wiser course be
to give Luther a warning, and to enlighten him rather
than to insult and irritate him? "The best way of coming to terms," he wrote to Cardinal Campeggio, "would
be for the pope to instruct each party to make a public
declaration of faith. By such a method the danger of
false statement would be overcome, and the wild talk

and exaggerated writings be mitigated." Again and
again he urged that a council be convoked, that a private
assembly be called together, and that the theses be discussed among scholars whose aim should be to bring the
matter to an issue "conformable with the spirit of Christianity."

But Rome paid as little attention to this warning
voice as to the wordy fireworks of Wittenberg. The
pope was busied with other cares than these: his beloved
Raphael Sanzio, the divinest gift of the Renaissance to
the new times, died suddenly at this juncture. Who
would now finish the Vatican cartoons? Who would
step forward to complete the decoration of St. Peter's,
a work so boldly conceived and so magnificently begun?
To the popes of the Medici family, art was greater and
more enduring and a hundredfold more important than
a pettifogging dispute among churchmen in an obscure
town in the province of Saxony; and precisely because
the reigning pope was a man of wide vision, he failed
to see the significance of the gesticulating little monk
who was busily undermining the papal realm. His cardinals, arrogant and self-confident—had they not a couple of decades earlier successfully committed Savonarola to the flames and ruthlessly expelled the heretics
from Spain?—insisted, however, that the edict against

Luther should be launched as the only suitable answer to the German zealot's insubordinate behaviour. Why should he first be given a hearing? Why bother any further about this peasant theologian? Erasmus's warning went unheeded; his letters were pigeon-holed and forgotten; the papal bull against Luther was issued; the legate was told to deal ruthlessly with the German insurgents: from the outset, obstinacy to the right, obstinacy to the left, made conciliation between the two camps impossible of achievement.

Yet in these decisive days—and hitherto historians have been prone to neglect the study of the background against which the events were enacted—the destiny of the German Reformation was for a while entirely in Erasmus's hands. Emperor Charles had summoned the Diet of Worms. Here the Luther affair was to be liquidated, unless he yielded at the eleventh hour. Frederick, the Elector of Saxony, Luther's liege-lord, was also invited, and though he did not as yet openly champion the reformer's cause he was resolved to give what protection he could. He was a strange fellow, this Elector of Saxony, for he was a faithful son of Mother Church, the greatest collector of relics and of bones of the saints in the whole of Germany, a respecter of things which

Luther scorned as baubles and devilish trickery, and yet he harboured sympathy for the reformer, he was proud of the man who had brought so much renown to the university of Wittenberg. Not having quite made up his mind which camp to enter, he kept prudently in the background and did not have personal dealings with Luther. As with Erasmus, so with Frederick: the elector did not receive the reformer, that in case of need he might be able to declare: "Personally, I have had nothing to do with him." From political motives, however, and because he saw that this vigorous peasant might well serve his turn in his schemes against the emperor, and, furthermore, out of particularist pride in his powers of jurisdiction, he had so far held a protective hand over Luther's head, so that in spite of papal pronouncements of outlawry the Augustinian continued to preach from the pulpit and still held his university chair.

At last, however, even this protection was imperilled, for, should the diet place Luther under the ban of the empire, then any further protection the elector should choose to offer would be looked upon as rebellion of a liege man against his suzerain. To an open breach of this kind none of the early half-Protestant princes were inclined to resort. They knew that from the military point of view the emperor was powerless, for his armies were in the field against France and Italy. Thus the moment might be propitious for increasing one's personal power and for striking a blow in the evangelical cause. History was unlikely to offer a more splendid opportunity. But Frederick, who was a pious and upright man, did not yet feel certain whether this priest and professor was in verity a herald of evangelical teaching or merely another of the numerous religious enthusiasts and sectarians. He could not decide whether before God and before earthly reason he could make himself further responsible in regard to this great and yet menacing spirit.

Such was Frederick's mood when, on his way through Cologne, he learned that Erasmus was staying in that city. He lost no time in dispatching Spalatinus, his secretary, to Erasmus's lodgings, to invite the famous humanist to an interview—for Erasmus was still looked upon as the highest moral authority in worldly and in theological matters, and he still enjoyed the honestly won reputation of being absolutely impartial. The elector expected to receive the wisest of counsels to allay his own uncertainty. He asked a straight question: Is Luther right or wrong? Such a question needed a straight answer. But Erasmus was not fond of Yes and No; especially was it inconvenient in this case, seeing the immense responsibility he would be taking upon himself.

If by his utterance he sanctioned Luther's deeds and words, then the elector, fortified by Erasmus's approval, would continue to shield his protégé, and the German Reformation would be saved. On the other hand, should Luther's liege lord decide to leave the disturber of the peace in the lurch, the latter's only course would be flight if he were to escape being burned alive. The destiny of a world swung on this Yes or No, and had Erasmus really been envious of or antagonistic to his great colleague, as many maintain that he was, now if ever he was given the chance to rid himself of a turbulent rival. A sharp, unconciliatory word would probably have decided the elector to withdraw his protection. On that day, November 5, 1520, the fate of the German Reformation, the whole future story of mankind, probably lay between Erasmus's delicate and timid hands.

Erasmus's attitude in that fateful hour was dignified and honourable. It was not a courageous attitude, nor a great, nor a decisive, nor a heroic attitude; but it certainly was an honourable one—and that is already something fine. When the elector asked him whether he considered Luther's outlook wrong-headed or heretical, Erasmus, determined not to take sides, said jestingly that Luther's main mistake had been to attack the pope by

threatening the tiara and the monks through laying
hands on their bellies. Then, having earnestly been besought to give a serious reply, he set forth his ideas concerning Luther's doctrines in twenty-two short propo-
sitions which he named *Axiomata*. Occasional sentences
ring a trifle censorious, such as "Luther misjudges the
leniency of the pope." But in the more important conclusions Erasmus stood courageously by the side of his
threatened colleague. "Among the many universities,
two only were found to condemn Luther, and even
these did not confute him. Luther was, therefore, only
demanding his due when he asked for an open discussion and unprejudiced judges." Again: "The best would
be for the pope to have the affair adjusted by trustworthy judges of good standing. The world is thirsting
after a true gospel, and the whole tendency of the day
is towards that. One should not go against the spirit of
the times in so spiteful a fashion." His concluding advice was that all parties should show themselves flexible,
that a public council should be summoned to discuss this
thorny problem before it led to a "tumultus" which
would unsettle the world for centuries to come.

With these words—for which Luther was by no
means as grateful as he might have been—a fresh turn
had been given to the Reformation, a turn which was

to its advantage. For though there are a few ambiguities and unduly guarded phrases in Erasmus's presentation, the elector acted precisely as Erasmus had proposed during that night's lengthy conversation. Next day, November 6, Frederick asked the papal legate to hold a public inquiry, to appoint trustworthy and unshackled judges, and not to have Luther's books burned before the matter had been thoroughly thrashed out. Simultaneously he entered a protest against the harsh standpoint of Rome and the emperor, thereby for the first time voicing the Protestantism of the German princes. By working behind the scenes, Erasmus was able in a weighty hour to give decisive help, and this secret intervention has earned him a monument rather than the stones which have been hurled against him

Followed the Diet of Worms, an epoch-making event. The town was full, every house packed to the roof and even to the tops of the gables to witness the entry of the young emperor, who had been crowned only a few months earlier. He was accompanied by legates, ambassadors, electors, secretaries, surrounded by the gaily hued accoutrements of riders and lansquenets. A few days later a monk entered by the same path, an insignificant fellow under the pope's ban, protected from being caught and burned at the stake by a letter of safe-conduct which lay carefully wrapped in his wallet. Yet once more the streets rang with shouts of joyous welcome. One of these men, the emperor, had been chosen by the princes as leader; the other had been elected to that position by the German nation.

At the first session the diet postponed the fateful decision. Erasmus's idea was still full of vitality, and a faint hope prevailed that some means of conciliation might be found. On the second day Luther uttered his famous "Here stand I; I can no otherwise." The world was rent in twain. For the first time since, more than a hundred years earlier, John Huss's defence before the Council of Constance, a man had faced the emperor and the court of Rome, and had refused to submit. A slight shiver ran through the assembly; they marvelled and wondered that a trumpery monk should dare to be so insubordinate. The common folk, however, gave Luther whole-hearted applause. Could they have already suspected such stubborn resistance to mean that a favourable wind was likely to start blowing in their direction? Could these stormy petrels have guessed that war was at hand?

But where was Erasmus during the hour of doom? It is tragical to relate that he was sitting tranquilly within the four walls of his study. He who had been

Jerome Aleander's friend in their young days, who had shared bed and board with him in Venice, he who had been persona grata with the recently crowned emperor, and was a sympathizer with evangelical views, was the only man who could have influenced the situation, and at least have obtained a postponement of sentence. But he dreaded a public appearance, and it was not until the evil tidings were brought to him that he realized the irrevocable nature of his lost opportunity. "If I had been present, I should have done the impossible, to prevent this tragedy occurring, and to bring about a moderate decision." But the decisive moments in history are never repeated. The absent are always wrong. Because in this dread hour Erasmus did not put his weight into the scale on the side of reform, did not, with the whole force of his personality, his powers, and his presence, influence the assembly, because he failed in this moment of utmost need, his own cause was lost for ever. Luther, however, fought his fight with the utmost courage and with unstinted strength; he put his whole heart into the defence: therefore was his will transformed into action.

STRUGGLE

FOR INDEPENDENCE

ERASMUS imagined—and most of his contemporaries shared his outlook—that the Diet of Worms, the ban of outlawry issued by the pope, and the ban of the empire proclaimed by the young emperor would have settled Luther's activities for ever. The only course that remained open was rebellion against Church and State, a new Albigensian or Waldensian or Hussite conflagration. This solution spelt war, and war was an activity Erasmus wanted above all to avoid. His dream had been to reform from within the evangelical teaching of Mother Church, and he would gladly have given his support to any movement of the kind he contemplated. "If Luther remains within the fold of the Church, I shall be happy to rally to his side," he declared in public. But with one blow and a wrench the fiery titan had severed his connexions with Rome. Erasmus's dream was at an end. "The Luther tragedy is finished. Ah, that it had never been staged!" Thus did

[173]

our lover of peace exclaim in the bitterness of his dis-
illusionment. The tiny flame of evangelical inquiry had
been snuffed out, the star of intellectual freedom had
set, "actum est de stellula lucis evangelicæ." Henceforward the familiars of the Inquisition and the heavy artil-
lery would have to decide the issue. Erasmus, feeling
himself too weak to stand so great a test, decided to
keep in the background of events. Humbly he recognized that he did not possess sufficient faith either in
God or in himself to take part in this vast and momentous struggle. "Zwingli and Bucer may be able to understand the language of the spirit, but Erasmus, being no
more than an ordinary mortal, is unable to learn this
tongue." Erasmus was now a man in his fifties, he had
long since realized that the problem concerning God
and things divine was an insoluble one, and he did not
feel called upon to be spokesman in the forthcoming
struggle. He desired to serve only in the realm where
clarity of mind held sway, he wished to serve the sciences and the arts. So he fled from theological discussion, from politics, from ecclesiastical wrangles, shut
himself up in his study, and amid the dignified silence
of his books he sought to ignore the noisy and unedify-
ing quarrels without. Here he could still be of use to the
world. Back, therefore, to your cell, Old Man, and cur-

tain your window against the vagaries of Time! Let others, who feel God's call echoing in their hearts, go forth to battle while you remain in tranquil security championing truth in the serene realm where art and science hold sway. "Even if the corrupt morals of the Roman clergy should demand a remedy out of the common, it is not for me and the likes of me to arrogate to ourselves the business of healers. I would rather suffer things to remain as they are than that through my intervention fresh unrest should arise, an unrest which often achieves quite the contrary of that which its moving spirits had set out to attain. Never have I, nor shall I, become an inciter to or a participator in an insurrection."

Thus Erasmus withdrew from the ecclesiastical hurly-burly into the serene domains of art, science, and his own work. He felt nauseated by the continued yapping and disputing of the factions. "Consulo quieti meæ," peace will I have, the "otium cum dignitate," the dignified ease of the scholar. But he reckoned without the world, and this refused to give him what he wanted. There are epochs wherein neutrality is stigmatized as a crime; during times of extreme political excitement the world insists upon a clear Yes or No, an affirmation of support or of disapproval, a distinct declaration of "I am for Luther or I am for the pope." The town of

Louvain, where he now lived, made it difficult for him to secure the peace he so greatly desired; and whereas Reformation Germany blamed him for his laodicean attitude towards Luther's teaching, the Catholic faculty of Louvain nicknamed him the promoter of the "Luther plague." The students, always champions of extremism, whether reactionary or revolutionary, made violent demonstrations against Erasmus, throwing down his chair at the university; meanwhile, from every pulpit in the town, the priests fulminated against him, and his former comrade Aleander, the papal legate, was hard put to it to bring this public condemnation to a close. Courage, as I have said before, was not one of Erasmus's virtues; he chose, therefore, to flee the city rather than to fight the issue. Just as in earlier days he had fled from the Black Death, so now did he flee from the hatred of the city where for many years he had carried on his labours. The old nomad packed his few belongings and started on his migrations once more. "I shall have to be careful not to let the Germans, who act as though they were possessed by the devil, tear me to pieces before I have shaken the dust of their empire off my feet." It has almost invariably been the lot of those who wish to keep outside the confines of partisanship to be driven into the medley.

Henceforward, Erasmus refused to live in any pronouncedly Catholic town or in one that had gone over to the side of the Reformation; his appropriate place was on neutral ground. He went to that perennial asylum of every independent spirit: Switzerland. For many years he stayed in Basle, the very heart of Europe, a quiet, dignified, and cleanly city, with well-kept streets, with sober and dispassionate inhabitants who paid no allegiance to war-mongering princes, but were democratically free. Here the scholar felt a promise of the serenity he longed for, here was an excellent university; here were colleagues of profound learning, friends who respected him, amanuenses to help him in his work, artists like Holbein; here, above all, was Frobenius the printer, the master-craftsman with whom for many years he had laboured happily side by side. The zeal of those whose pleasure it was to serve him procured him a comfortable house, and for the first time this man of many wanderings found himself installed in something like a home, in a free city where it was delightful to dwell. Here he could live the life of the spirit; this was his true, his real world. Only in such places, where he could write his books undisturbed, only in such places, where these works could be finely and carefully printed, could he feel genuinely happy. Basle became the resting-house of his earthly pilgrimage. He lived in this town longer than in any other, a whole eight years, and with the passage of time the two names, Erasmus and Basle, have become inseparable: one cannot nowadays think of Erasmus without calling up the vision of Basle, or of Basle without picturing Erasmus. His house is still kept intact and preciously conserved, the walls hung with some of Holbein's portraits of the sage which will carry his lineaments down to countless generations to come. In this abode most of Erasmus's finest works were written, above all the *Colloquia*, that sparkling Latin dialogue which was first conceived as a primer for young Frobenius, and was destined to become a Latin textbook for innumerable children during future decades. Here he completed his great edition of the Fathers of the Church, and hence he sent letters to all the corners of the earth. Here, entrenched in the citadel of work, he could pursue his labours, untroubled by the clamour without; book after book issued from his pen, and when intellectual Europe wished to look upon its leader it gazed upon the regal city on the farther shores of the Rhine. During the period of Erasmus's residence there, Basle became the intellectual alsatia. Humanistic pupils gathered round the celebrated scholar, Œcolampadius for instance, Rhenanus, Amerbach. No man of note, no prince, no scholar, no friend of the fine arts, ever missed seeking out Erasmus in Frobenius's printing-press or in his house "Zum Lufft"; pilgrims journeyed from France and Germany and Italy in order to see the man they honoured, and watch him at his work. While in Wittenberg and Zurich and at all the other universities the theological warfare raged and stormed, here in this city calm prevailed. It seemed to have become the last refuge of the arts and sciences.

Old man, do not deceive yourself, your real day has set, your realm has been ravaged and destroyed. The true combat is outside your study walls; it is a life-and-death struggle; the spirit has become biased, and the opponents have joined battle: a free man, a man of independent mind, a man who holds aloof, can no longer be tolerated. The world war rages and you needs must be either for or against the evangelical renewal; it no longer helps you to sit among your books behind closed windows. Now that, from one end of Europe to the other, Luther has split the Christian world in twain, it behoves you to cease hiding your head in the sand; no longer can you evade the issue by making the childish excuse, "I have not read your books." To right and to left the ominous words ring forth: "Who is not for us is against us." When a cosmos is riven, the rift is felt in every human heart. No, Erasmus, it no longer saves you to take to your heels, and soon you will be dislodged from your citadel. The times need men who are not afraid to state their beliefs frankly; the world wishes to know where Erasmus, its intellectual leader, stands; whether he is for Luther or against him, whether he is for the pope or against him.

A shattering drama is about to fill the stage. The world's ardent desire is to get hold of a man weary of war, and to drag him into the struggle. "It is a misfortune," laments Erasmus at the age of fifty-five, "that this worldwide storm should have caught me unprepared, should have overtaken me at the moment when, weary from my manifold labours, I was looking forward to a period of well-earned rest. Why can I not be allowed to remain an onlooker at this tragedy, for participation in which I feel so ill adapted? Why are they trying to thrust me into a part, when there are so many other people who would gladly appear upon the stage?" At such critical times fame imposes obligations that make it a curse rather than a blessing; an Erasmus is too vividly in the public eye, what he says is too important, for the members of either party, be it left or right, to forgo the possibility of consulting him as an authority.

The leaders on both fronts tore and tugged in order to win him to their particular cause. They lured him with offers of money, with flattery; they taunted him for cowardice, hoping thereby to induce him to break his prudent silence; they alarmed him with false reports, saying that in Rome his books had been confiscated and burned; they falsified his letters; they twisted the meaning of his words. In such circumstances, the true worth of a man of independent mind shines brightly forth. Emperor, kings, three popes on one side, while on the other were Luther, Melanchthon, and Zwingli—all urging Erasmus to speak the decisive word. Anything he wished for on this earth would be granted him, if only he would throw in his lot with one party or the other. He knew that he could have taken his place "in the leading ranks of the Reformation party" if only he would make a clear statement that he was of their way of thinking; he knew, equally well, that he could have been "nominated to a bishopric" if he had consented to write an attack upon Luther. But Erasmus's thoroughly honourable nature revolted against such unqualified and one-sided statements. He could not with a clear conscience champion the cause of the papal Church since he had been one of the first among men then living to shed light upon its abuses, to demand its reform from within; but to the evangelicals neither could he give whole-hearted allegiance, since they were not conveying to the world his idea of a Christ of peace, but had gone violently to work. "Continuously they clamour, 'Evangelium, Evangelium!' They alone are to act as interpreters! At one time the Gospels made the savage gentle, robbers benevolent, the quarrelsome peace-loving; those that cursed were converted so that they invoked blessings. But these men, as if possessed, start all kinds of insurrections, and speak evil of many who deserve better. I see before me new impostors and hypocrites, new tyrants, but not a spark of the evangelical spirit." No, to neither party, were it the pope's or were it Luther's, would Erasmus consent to give in his adhesion. Peace, peace alone, peace, and again peace; only to be allowed to stand quietly aside, to be able to continue his work of promoting the welfare of mankind. "Consulo quieti meæ."

But Erasmus's fame was too widespread and the waiting for his confession of faith too eager. From every point of the compass he was implored to come forth and speak the words that would decide the issue for himself and for all the world. To show how profound was the general belief in his integrity, I need but quote a moving appeal from the very heart of one of the noblest of Germans. Albrecht Dürer, while travelling in the Netherlands, had made Erasmus's acquaintance. When, a few months later, it was bruited abroad that Luther's cause was dead, Dürer looked to Erasmus as the only man alive who was worthy to carry the sacred cause a stage further, and, shaken to the soul, he apostrophized the sage: "O Erasme Roterdame, where art thou? Hear, thou Christian knight; thou must ride forth shoulder to shoulder with the Lord Christ to defend the truth and to earn a martyr's crown. Otherwise thou art nothing but a petty old man. I myself have heard thee say that thou hast a couple of years' good life still in thee and that thou intendest to do something. Well, why not give these two last years to the evangel, to the true Christian belief in God? Let thy voice be heard, then the doors of hell, the papal chair, as Christ says, cannot prevail against thee. Bestir thyself, Erasmus, that thou mayest overthrow Goliath, to become the man after God's own heart, as did David of old."

Thus thought Dürer together with the whole of Germany. No less did the Catholic Church set her hopes on Erasmus in her deadly need, and Christ's representative on earth, the pope himself, wrote a letter couched in almost identical terms. "Step forth, step forth and support Christ's cause! Use your wonderful gifts to God's honour and glory. Bethink you that, with God's aid, you are capable of winning back most of those who have been led astray by Luther, setting their feet once more in the right path, of securing that all those who have not yet been seduced shall remain steadfast, and of persuading those who are about to stray to remain within the fold." The lord of Christendom and his bishops; the rulers of the world, Henry VIII of England, Charles V, Francis I of France, Ferdinand of Austria, and the Duke of Burgundy, were on one side—while on the other were the leaders of the Reformation, every one of them beseeching Erasmus, as during the Trojan war did Homeric princes outside the tent of the sulky Achilles, to bestir himself, to come out of his lethargy and enter arena. The scene is majestically set. Seldom, indeed, have the mighty of the earth struggled for an utterance from one single individual, seldom has the supremacy of the mind been so victoriously manifested. But we have to realize the hidden cleavage in Erasmus's character. Never did he give these wooers who hung upon his every word a definite and heroic "I will not." He could not muster strength enough for an open, decisive, and unambiguous pronouncement. With neither party did he care to throw in his lot—and this, after all, does him credit, for it proves his spiritual independence. The unfortunate thing was, however, that he also did not wish to be in either party's bad graces, and that deprives his attitude of dignity. He dared not enter into open opposition with any of these persons of importance, all of whom were his benefactors or his admirers or his supporters, so he fobbed them off with evasions and divagations; he tried to side-track them, he temporized, he caracoled—how can one describe the unsatisfactoriness of his behaviour except by the use of some such words as these?—promising and hesitating, writing down binding words which failed to bind him, flattering and dissembling, excusing himself by saying he was sick, or tired, or explaining his reluctance by maintaining that he was incompetent to judge. To the pope he wrote with exaggerated modesty. How could he, so scantily furnished with intellectual endowments, he whose education had been so mediocre, how could he presume to undertake so enormous a task as the extirpation of heresy? The King of England was put off with some fresh excuse month after month, year after year; and Erasmus resorted to the same methods in his dealings with Melanchthon and Zwingli, temporizing with them in flattering epistles. He knew hundreds of ways of wriggling out of his difficulty. And yet behind this unpleasing façade of machinations there was hidden a resolute will. "If there be a man who cannot esteem Erasmus because he appears to be an unreliable Christian, let him think what he will of me. I cannot be other than I am. If Christ has endowed another with rarer mental powers, and this better-gifted person feels more sure of himself than I do, let him use these advantages to the better glory of the Lord. My reason tells me to take my way along a quieter and less dangerous road. I cannot help it if I hate discord and division, while loving peace and mutual understanding, for I have long since realized how dark and complicated are all human affairs. I know how much easier it is to incite to disorder than to damp down such disorder once it is let loose. And since I do not trust my own reason in all things, I prefer to step aside and not force myself to agree or to disagree with another man's mode of thought. My one wish is that all of us should unite to bring about the victory of the Christian cause and the triumph of that peace which is spoken of in the Gospels, to bring this about without violence, and by means of truth and reasonableness, so that in the end we shall understand one another perfectly, both as to priestly dignity and the freedom of the people whom our Lord Jesus Christ desired to see free. All those who, according to their capacities, will work towards this goal will have Erasmus as comrade in the fight. But if any should wish to drag me into the confusion, for him Erasmus will be neither a leader nor a companion."

His resolution was unshakable, and so he kept pope, emperor, kings, and reformers like Luther, Melanchthon, and Dürer, waiting year after year, and none of them was able ever to force from his lips the decisive word they expected. He smiled politely down upon his interlocutors, but his mouth remained sealed for ever.

But there was one man alive who refused to wait, an ardent and impatient warrior in the spirit's cause, resolute in his determination to cut this Gordian knot. This doughty knight was named Ulrich von Hutten, the "Knight who fought against Death and the Devil," the Archangel Michael of the German Reformation. He had looked up to Erasmus as to a father, trustingly and lovingly. Passionately devoted to humanistic ideas, the young man's most heartfelt desire was that he might become "the Alcibiades of this new Socrates"; he had laid his very life in Erasmus's hands, "in summa, if the Gods vouchsafe it to me, and if you are long spared to be the honour of Germany, I am willing to leave all in order to be at your side." Erasmus, who was invariably susceptible to admiration, reciprocated by joyfully accepting this "peculiar lover of the Muses," for he delighted in the glowing youth of the man who had sung rapturously like a lark at heaven's gate, "O sæculum, O litteræ! Juvat vivere!" How confident is this exclamation, "It is a joy to be alive!" Erasmus had hoped to train the stripling to solid scholarship and to make of him a new master of the sciences. Soon, however, political activities had severed pupil from teacher; the airless rooms and the bookish knowledge of the humanists became too confined for Hutten. The young knight, son of a knight, drew the gauntlet on once more; he no longer wanted to wield the pen but a sword against pope and clerics. Although he had won his laureate's crown for Latin verse, he flung this foreign tongue aside in order that he might in the German vernacular summon his fellows to the fight for German evangelical teaching:

> In Latin did I often write—
> This was not known to everyone.
> Now call I to my fatherland.

But Germany would not tolerate him and drove him forth; in Rome he barely escaped arrest and assassination. Banished from home and from court, a beggar and prematurely old, undermined in health by the "malady of France" (as syphilis was then called), covered with sores, with the last strength at his command he dragged himself to Basle. He was thirty-five years old. In Basle lived his great friend, the "Light of Germany," his teacher, his master, his protector: Erasmus. The young poet had helped to spread the sage's fame; the friendship of this scholar had accompanied him on his wanderings; letters of recommendation from Erasmus had opened many a door to him; indeed, he owed much of his facility for versification (now greatly reduced and half decayed) to Erasmus's guidance. So, in his ultimate necessity, just before the end, Hutten turned to his sometime friend.

And Erasmus? Never had his unfortunate anxiety of mind shown itself to such disadvantage as under this soul-shattering test. Erasmus refused to admit Hutten to his house. Already in Louvain, Erasmus had found this "quarrelsome brawler" very hard to stomach; and when the poet had urged his master to declare war on the clergy, Erasmus had curtly declared: "My business is to further the cause of education." Now he felt no inclination to receive the fanatic who had sacrificed the Muse of poetry upon the altar of politics; he would have nothing to do with this "Pylades of Luther"—anyway not openly, and especially not in this city where he was spied upon by hundreds of eyes. Erasmus was genuinely frightened by the advent of the unmercifully hunted, dying creature. He had three reasons for being afraid: first, because of the man's physical condition, which was appalling (Erasmus had invariably decamped whenever the plague was about in his neighbourhood, he having a phobia concerning infection); secondly, because he dreaded lest this "egens et omnibus rebus destitutus," this beggar who had lost everything he possessed, might ask for shelter beneath Erasmus's roof and remain to be a pecuniary burden for the rest of his life; and, thirdly, because the fellow who had ventured to admonish the pope and had incited the German nation to take up arms against the priesthood might compromise the attitude of non-partisanship Erasmus had adopted. He turned Hutten from his door, not with a definite "I don't want you," but, following the dictates of his nature, with pettifogging excuses, such as that he could not on account of his stone trouble and his colics receive Hutten in a warmed room (an essential to the sorely afflicted poet) since stove-heating was quite unbearable to him—an obvious, a pitiful subterfuge.

A drama which put all spectators to the blush was now enacted. Basle, which was at that time a small town comprising no more than a hundred streets and two or three squares, where everyone knew his neighbours, witnessed the painful sight of Ulrich von Hutten, a knight, one of the champions of Luther, a famous poet, limping about its alleyways, slouching into beer-houses, passing again and again in front of the home where his former friend lived, his friend who had been the first to awaken him to the magnificence of the evangelical cause. Sometimes Hutten stood in the market-place looking with angry eyes at the locked door and the carefully shuttered windows of the man who had once named him "the new Lucian," and had proclaimed him to be the greatest satirical writer of the day. Like a snail in its shell, Erasmus sat huddled in the security of his house, an old and scraggy man, fuming with impatience for the departure of this disturber of the peace, "this burdensome vagrant." Why does not the pestiferous fellow leave the city? Underground messages hastened to and fro, and still Hutten waited, still he hoped to see the door open, and the hand of his friend stretched forward to help him in his misery. But Erasmus kept silent, and, though his conscience was uneasy, he lay hidden in his own house.

At length Hutten left, his poisoned body now harbouring within it a poisoned heart. He dragged himself to Zurich, where Zwingli gave him a welcome, helped him financially, and found him a quiet refuge on the little isle of Ufenau in Lake Zurich. Hutten was nearing his end and was kept most of the time ill in bed, until he died, and was laid to rest in the islet that had sheltered his frail and worn-out body. But before he breathed his last, this Chevalier sans Peur et sans Reproche once more raised his almost shattered sword in order, though only with the stump, to deal Erasmus a mortal blow, Erasmus the man of faith who was too cautious to proclaim his faith aloud. In a terrific indictment—*Expostulatio cum Erasmo*—he belaboured his former friend and leader. He depicted the pusillanimous scholar as an insatiable fame-hunter, as envious of the growing renown of another (a shrewd blow for Luther's camp), accused him of fickleness, poured ridicule upon his weaknesses, crying aloud so that the whole of Germany should hear the words: "Though Erasmus is in the bottom of his heart at one with the evangelical cause, he has shamefully betrayed it." From the death-bed Hutten summoned Erasmus before a world tribunal, to show his colours, to declare himself against the Reformation since he had not the courage to come forth as its advocate. Among the evangelicals Erasmus was no longer feared. "Gird yourself, the cause is ripe for ac-

tion, and this would be a deed worthy of your advanced
years. Gather all your energies and turn them into this
work—you will find your opponent fully armed. The
Lutheran party, which you would fain wipe from the
face of the earth, is awaiting the combat and will not
fail to join battle." Knowing full well the division in
Erasmus's nature, Hutten told him frankly: "You will
not be equal to such a fight as this, for your conscience
warns you that on many points you agree with Luther.
Part of you will not be able to attack us vigorously because in reality you will have to attack your own earlier
writings; you will be obliged to turn your knowledge
against yourself, and eloquently to forswear your former eloquence. Your own books will have to fight
against one another."

Erasmus knew at once that the blow had gone home.
So far only insignificant scribblers had assaulted him.
Time and again some peevish penman had drawn his
attention to a mistranslation; and these petty wasp-
stings had hurt his sensitive soul. Now he was being
attacked by a doughtier foe, who battered him, and
summoned him to declare himself before the whole
German nation. In the first hours of alarm he endeavoured to suppress the manuscript which (in many
copies) was circulating from hand to hand; but, since

this manœuvre proved unsuccessful, he wrathfully seized his pen and answered in his *Spongia adversus Aspergines Hutteni* (Sponge to wipe out Hutten's aspersions). He rendered blow for blow; nor, though he knew that Hutten was wounded unto death, did he shrink from hitting below the belt. In four hundred and twenty-four separate clauses, he nailed one accusation after another, and concluded with a magnificent and unambiguous confession of faith—for he was always great when his foundation, his independence, was assailed. "In many books, in many letters, in many disputations, I have unfalteringly declared that I refuse to mix myself in the affairs of any party whatsoever. When Hutten rails against me because I have not rallied to Luther's support, as he himself would have me do, he fails to remember how three years ago I explicitly asserted that the Lutheran party was alien to my outlook and that it would always remain so; I even added that not only did I myself wish to keep out of it, but that I encouraged my friends to do likewise. I cannot change from this position. By the Lutheran party I mean the group of persons who whole-heartedly accept all that Luther has written or is writing or will write at some future date. Such abasement may be witnessed among even the most competent and worthy men; but for my part I have said frequently to my friends that, if the Lutherans could feel kindly to me only on condition that I should agree unreservedly with their tenets, let them think what they will, I cannot do so. I love freedom, and I will not and cannot serve any party."

The vigorous counter-attack never touched Ulrich von Hutten. By the time it was printed and put into circulation, the dauntless fighter had gone to his long rest where the gentle lapping of the waves lulled him in his lonely grave. Death had conquered Hutten before the mortal blow launched by Erasmus could reach him. But even in death, Hutten, the mighty defeated, gained one final victory. He achieved what neither emperor nor kings, what neither pope nor clergy with all the power of authority behind them, had been able to achieve; his biting sarcasms had drawn Erasmus from his lair. For, having publicly been held up to ridicule on account of his poltroonery and vacillation, Erasmus was forced to demonstrate that he was not afraid of a scuffle with the greatest of his antagonists, with Luther himself. He had now to "show his colours," he had now to take a side. It was with a heavy heart that Erasmus set to work. He was an old man who desired nothing more from life than peace and tranquillity. Nor was he

deceived as to the position in respect of Luther's cause;
he knew that it had long since become too powerful to
be shuffled out of existence with a stroke of the pen. He
knew that no one would be convinced by his eloquence,
that he could change nothing, and better nothing. Lacking pleasure in, lacking any desire for, the undertaking,
he entered the battle which had been thrust upon him.
He could not draw back now. And when his work
against Luther was at length, in 1524, handed over to
the printer, he sighed, relieved at heart: "Jacta alea est"
(the die is cast).

SETTLEMENT OF
ACCOUNTS

LITERARY gossip is not peculiar to one epoch; it is with us always. Even in the sixteenth century, when men of learning were but thinly strewn over the land, nothing could be kept secret from these inquisitives. Before Erasmus had taken his pen in hand, before even he was certain that he would enter the fray, they knew in Wittenberg what had been planned in Basle. Luther was counting upon the attack. "Truth is mightier than eloquence," he had written to a friend in 1522, "and faith is greater than erudition. I shall never issue a challenge to Erasmus, nor do I intend, should he attack me, immediately to defend myself. I should prefer, indeed, that he should not shoot the bolts of his eloquence at me . . . if, nevertheless, he should venture to do so, he will learn that Christ fears neither the portals of hell nor the powers of the air. I shall pick up the famous Erasmus's gauntlet, and shall give battle without any consideration as to his reputation, his name, or his standing."

This letter, which Luther obviously wished to have communicated to Erasmus, was a threat, or at least a warning. Behind the bluff words one cannot but feel that at bottom Luther would have preferred to avoid a clash of pens, seeing the critical moment he was then traversing. In both camps, therefore, friends of the belligerents took a hand in the game, hoping to act as mediators. Melanchthon and Zwingli both endeavoured, in the good cause of evangelical teaching, to bring about a reconciliation between Basle and Wittenberg; and at the outset their intermediation seemed most promising. Then, unexpectedly, Luther made up his mind to address Erasmus personally.

But how greatly had his tone changed since, a few years earlier, Luther had written to "the great man" in polite, nay, overpolite, terms, in the spirit of a pupil towards a master. He now realized that a historic hour was about to chime, he likewise had become fully aware what his mission was to be, and his words, therefore, had a passionate clangour. What was one foe more or less to Luther, who was at war with pope and emperor, indeed with all the powers of the earth? He was sick of secret machinations. He refused to form a pact with uncertainty and lukewarmness. "I will have neither part nor lot with vague and faltering words or speeches."

Luther wanted clarity. For the last time he held a hand out to Erasmus, making an offer of reconciliation—but the hand was already wearing an iron gauntlet.

The opening words of this missive are polite and restrained. "I have been sitting quiet long enough, my dear Herr Erasmus, and though I have been waiting for you, as the greater man and the elder of us twain, to make the first move to break the silence between us, yet after so long a wait, my love urges me to make a beginning myself, by writing to you. I have no objections to make in regard to your dealings with the pope, if you yourself are satisfied. . . ." Then, in mighty and always disdainful words, the writer's ill-humour against the shilly-shallier breaks forth: "For since it is obvious that the Lord has not yet endowed you with such constancy, such courage, and such sense, as should lead you to fight against this monster boldly, shoulder to shoulder with us, I would not expect of you what is too much for my own strength. . . . I should, however, have preferred it had you thought fit to refrain from devoting your gifts to mingling in our affairs; for although, with your standing and your eloquence, you might achieve much, yet it would be better, since your heart is not with us, for you to serve God only with the talent he confided to your safe keeping." He goes on to regret

Erasmus's weaknesses and aloofness, then, in the end, he hurls forth the decisive word, crying that the importance of the matter had now far outstretched Erasmus's goal, that there it would not endanger him (Luther) if Erasmus should put his whole weight in the balance against the Lutheran cause, and still less could an occasional sneer or gibe do any hurt. Arrogantly and almost dictatorially, he challenged Erasmus to forbear the use of "biting, rhetorical, and flowery language," and, above all, if he could do nothing else, to remain "an onlooker upon the tragedy" and not to encourage the other side. Erasmus was not to attack Luther in writings, and Luther for his part would refrain taking up his pen against Erasmus. "There has been enough biting; we must now see to it that we do not tear one another to pieces and destroy each other."

Such high-handed letters had never come Erasmus's way. The prince of the humanistic realm, despite his serenity of mind, could not endure that the man who had of yore addressed him so humbly, asking for protection, should now challenge him so derogatorily, treating him as a babbler of no importance. So he answered proudly: "I have worked better on behalf of evangelical teaching than many who now plume themselves upon their knowledge of the Gospels. I see, also, that this Reformation has brought into being many corrupt and insurrectionary men, and I see that the apostles of humane letters are prone to walk backwards like a crab, that friendships are being broken, and I fear lest a bloodstained revolt may occur. I shall never admit that the evangel shall be sacrificed on the altar of human passion." He emphasized the fact that, had he chosen to come forth against Luther, he would have gained the thanks and approbation of the mighty. But perhaps one did better service to the cause of the Gospels by entering the field against Luther than did those fools who so loudly clamoured in his name and on account of whom it was impossible to remain merely an onlooker at the tragedy. Luther's uncompromising attitude had hardened Erasmus's wavering will. "Ah, that it may not end in tragedy," he moaned in vague anticipation. Then he took up his pen, his only weapon, once again.

Erasmus knew very well that his opponent was a titan; at the bottom of his heart he may also have realized Luther's superiority as a fighter, and the vigour of his rages against which no opposition seemed able to prevail. But Erasmus's strength lay in the fact that he knew his own limitations, and this is very rare in a man of artistic temperament. He knew that the intellectual tourney was being played before the eyes of the whole world, and that the theologists and the humanists of Europe were eagerly awaiting the issue of the jousts. It was necessary, therefore, to occupy an impregnable position, and Erasmus chose one with masterly cunning. He did not run atilt against Luther head down, blindly hoping to unsaddle him, but sought with the eye of a hawk for the vulnerable points in Lutheran teaching, choosing, apparently, a side issue, though it was in reality the very core of Luther's doctrinal edifice—which was still wobbly upon its foundations and far as yet from being complete. Even Luther was forced "to praise and to extol" this selection: "You among all my opponents have seized upon the kernel of the matter; you are the one and only man who has beheld the vital nerve of the subject at issue, and who has in this struggle taken the matter by the throat." With his amazing power of penetration, Erasmus selected in this hand-to-hand encounter not the firm foothold of conviction, but, rather, the slippery dialectical ground of a question in theology upon which the iron-fisted opponent was unable to strike him to earth, and in which he knew that he would have the invisible backing and protection of the philosophers of every epoch.

The problem selected by Erasmus as the basis of discussion has been a bone of contention among theologians down the ages: the question of the freedom or the non-freedom of the human will. Luther, following the traditional Augustinian teaching of predestination, maintained that man remained for ever God's captive. He possesses not an iota of free will; every action he performs is known by God beforehand and is traced out by divine ordinance. By no good works, by no "bona opera," by no contrition, is man able to put his own will in motion, to liberate himself from the entanglement caused by antecedent sin; God's grace alone is competent to lead man along the right path. In modern phraseology we should say: our individual destiny is governed entirely by the massive bulk of our heredity, by concatenations of circumstance which no personal will can control insofar as God does not will it. As Goethe says:

> . . . Volition
> Is naught but willing what we have to will.

Naturally a humanist who believed in the human reason as a sacred and God-given power, could not accept such a doctrine. Erasmus was unshaken in his belief that not only individual men, but the whole of mankind, could, by an upright and disciplined exertion of the will, be raised to a higher level of morality; so that to him such a stark and almost Mohammedan fatalism must have been profoundly uncongenial. But Erasmus would not have been Erasmus if he had uttered a frank and downright No to the opinions of a rival. Here as elsewhere he shrank from extremes, and could not see his way to accepting Luther's curt and uncompromisingly determinist outlook. He himself admitted, in his cautious and vacillating way, that he took "no pleasure in definite assertions"; his inclination was towards doubt; and he gladly submitted in such cases to the words of the Scriptures and of Mother Church. In Holy Writ ideas were often expressed in an obscure way and were not thoroughly explained. On this account he felt that it was dangerous to declare as resolutely as did Luther that there was no such thing as free will. He did not say that Luther's concept was wholly false, but he objected to the adoption of so uncompromising an attitude as was expressed in the phrase "non nihil"; he refused to accept the contention that all the good works a man performs can make no impression on God and are, therefore, superfluous. If, as Luther did, one attributed everything to God's grace, what sense was there in men trying to do good? One should (again we hear the man who ever has a foot in both camps) at least leave the illusion of free will to man, so that he sink not into despair, and so that God may not seem to him cruel and unjust. "I agree with those who attribute certain things to free will and the majority of things to the grace of God, for we must not in this matter avoid the Scylla of pride and thereby fall upon the Charybdis of fatalism."

Even when the battle was joined, Erasmus, the peacemaker, went a long way to meet his opponent. He took occasion to warn his contemporaries not to place too great importance upon such discussions, but, rather, "to ask themselves if it is right to set the whole world in a conflagration for the sake of a few paradoxical conceptions." If only Luther would yield but the fraction of an inch, would but take one step to meet him, this intellectual squabble would end in peace and harmony. But could Erasmus hope for compromise from the most iron-minded man of that century, from a man who in matters of belief and conviction would not, even if tied to the stake, sacrifice a jot or tittle of his principles, who, born fanatic that he was, would prefer death or the destruction of the world to giving up the tiniest and most indifferent paragraph of his doctrines?

Luther did not answer Erasmus at once, although this man of wrath and violence was irritated in the extreme by the attack. "While I cared not a rap for and did not

· even trouble to peruse the other books in which I have been taken to task, I read the Erasmian document, but all the time I was reading I felt inclined to fling the thing into the fire," he exclaimed roughly, after his customary fashion. But during the year 1524 weightier and more important affairs pressed upon him, matters of far greater urgency than a theological discussion. The fate of every revolutionary is that he, who wishes to replace the old order by the new, has to let loose the forces of chaos, and he risks being outstripped by others yet more radical than he, who will make confusion worse confounded. Luther had demanded freedom of speech and religion; now his followers began making demands on their own account: the Zwickau prophets, Karlstadt, Münzer, "all these gushers," as Luther called them, had rallied under the banner of evangelical reform to defy the emperor and the realm. Luther's own words against the nobles and the princes were converted by these allies into pikes and caltrops; what he had intended to be a religious and spiritual revolution was, in the hands of an oppressed peasantry, becoming a social and communist insurrection. During these trying days the spiritual tragedy of Erasmus was repeated with Luther; world-shaking events he had never desired came to pass because of his words, and, just as he had reproached

Erasmus for being a Laodicean, so now did the folk of the "Bundschuh," the cloister-stormers and the image-breakers, reprove him for being "a new-fangled papistical sophist," the "friend of Antichrist," and "the uppish flesh of Wittenberg." Erasmus's fate! What he had meant to be taken in a spiritual sense was interpreted literally by the masses and their fanatical leaders, so that, as he said, his words became "fleshly," and took on a crude agitational colour. The same fate befalls every revolution; one wave succeeds another. If Erasmus may be likened to the Girondists, then Luther may be compared with the Jacobins, and Thomas Münzer and his followers with the ultra-Jacobins such as Marat. He, who had hitherto been undisputed leader, had suddenly to carry on the fight along two fronts simultaneously, against the lukewarm and against the wild men of the woods; he must bear full responsibility for the social revolution, for the most horrible and most bloodstained insurrection Germany had experienced for centuries. For it was his name that was inscribed in the heart of the commonalty. It was his incendiary action against emperor and empire which gave these minor incendiaries the pluck to rise against their counts and lieges. "We are harvesting the fruit of your mind," Erasmus could call to him, and the reproach was fully justified.

"You refuse to acknowledge your acquaintance with the rebels, but they recognize you well enough. You can do nothing to prevent public opinion from ascribing present events to the influence of your books, especially those written in the German tongue."

Luther was faced with a terrible dilemma: was he, whose roots went deep into the folk-life and whose own existence linked him so intimately with the peasantry which he had summoned to revolt against the princes, now to repudiate those who were fighting along the path he had pointed out, those who, at his summons, and in the name of evangelical freedom, had become disloyal to the princes? For the first time in his life (his situation having suddenly changed to something extraordinarily similar to that of Erasmus) Luther endeavoured to deal with the crisis "Erasmically." He warned the princes to exercise moderation, he warned the peasantry not "to bring disgrace upon the name of Christianity by deeds of violence, by impatience, and unchristianly behaviour." But—and this was a terrible blow to a man equipped with Luther's colossal self-confidence—the common people no longer hearkened to his voice, but, rather, to those who promised them most, to Thomas Münzer and the communistic theologians. In the end he was forced to a decision, for the unbridled upheaval threatened to compromise his work; and he realized that the internecine struggle would hamper his own spiritual fight against the papacy. "If these murderous spirits had not drawn the peasants into their nets, things would now have been otherwise with the papacy." When his work and his mission were at stake, Luther never hesitated. Himself a revolutionary, he had nevertheless to take his stand against the peasant revolution; and when Luther took sides he could only do so as an extremist, in the wildest, most biased, most ferocious way imaginable. Among all his writings, the one which was the child of this hour of danger, his pamphlet against the German peasantry, is the most bloodthirsty and terrific. "Those who rally to the side of the princes will become holy martyrs; those who fail, will go to the devil; therefore let all who can, both in public and in private, strike down and strangle these miscreants —bearing ever in mind that there is nothing more poisonous, more noisome, more devilish, than a man who incites the people to insurrection." Without stopping to consider, he ranged himself with authority and against the people. "The donkey needs a thrashing, and the brute populace must be governed by brute force." Not a word did this berserker find to say on behalf of clemency when the conquering knighthood suppressed the peasant revolt with abominable ruthlessness; he had no pity for the innumerable victims, for in his wrath he knew no measure; not a syllable would he utter on behalf of the thousands who had put their trust in him, and who had been initiated by him into the art of insurrection against their overlords. In the end he acknowledged with a grim courage, when the fields of Württemberg were running with blood: "I, Martin Luther, have slain all the peasants who died during this rebellion, for I goaded authority to the slaughter. Their blood be on my head."

This "furor," this tremendous power for hating, still whetted his quill when he turned it against Erasmus in his reply. He might have forgiven his rival's theological excursus, but the enthusiastic welcome given to it in the wide realm of humanistic culture fanned the flames of his wrath till it became raving madness. Luther winced at the notion that his enemies were intoning a song of triumph. "Tell me, where is the doughty Maccabæus, where is he who is so sure of his teaching?" Now that the peasant trouble lay behind him, he would not only answer Erasmus, but crush him out of existence. While at board with some friends he made known his intention in the awesome announcement: "I conjure you, therefore, at God's command, to become Erasmus's vowed foes and that you have naught to do with his books. I shall write all I have it in mind to say no matter if he dies of it and rots. I intend to kill Satan with my pen." To which he added, not without a tincture of pride: "Just as I slew Münzer, whose blood is on my head."

But even in his rages and precisely when his blood was at boiling-point, Luther, as artist and man of genius, was never false to the German language. He knew how formidable was his antagonist, and, conscious of this, his work took on the proportions of greatness. It was a book on the grand scale, going to the root of things, of a wide compass, sparkling with images, glowing with passion, a book which, in addition to its vast erudition, displays more magnificently than any of his other works his imaginative and human powers. *De servo arbitrio* (a treatise upon the servitude of the will) is one of the greatest compositions in the realm of controversial literature that this firebrand ever wrote. Thanks to it, the settlement of accounts with Erasmus has become one of the most significant discussions ever engaged in by two men of utterly opposing temperaments. No matter how far from our present interests the subject may now appear, because of the magnitude of the parties ranged against one another it has become one of the greatest achievements in the whole domain of literature.

Before Luther entered the lists, before buckling his harness and pulling down his visor, before taking spear in hand for a murderous thrust, he raised for a moment, but only for a brief moment, his weapon in courtly salutation. "I give you honour and praise such as I have never given you before." He recognized straightforwardly that Erasmus had dealt with him "gently and with consideration," and had been the only one to touch the nerve of the whole issue. But no sooner was the salute made than he clenched his fist resolutely, became rude, and was immediately in his own proper element. He answered Erasmus, so he said, because St. Paul had commanded that "vain talkers must have their mouths stopped." Blow followed upon blow. With magnificent, truly Luther-like imagery, he hammered away at Erasmus with all his might, reproaching him for that he was always walking on eggs, never wishing to crush one, was always stepping between glasses and never touching one. Mockingly he declared: "Erasmus refuses to stand his ground on any issue, and yet he maintains such a judgment concerning us—that is as good as running to avoid a slight shower and tumbling into a pond." At a stroke he revealed the contrast between Erasmus's stealthy prudence and his own unambiguous directness and certitude. The former deemed bodily freedom, comfort, and peace higher assets than belief, whereas he himself was ready to believe even though the whole world should be filled with unrest and should sink into decay and ruin. Since Erasmus in his attack warned him to be cautious and quoted certain ambiguities in the biblical texts, dubious points which no mortal should venture to interpret with absolute confidence and self-assuredness, Luther yelled: "Without certitude, Christianity cannot exist. A Christian must be sure of his doctrine and his cause, or he is no Christian." He who hesitates, is lukewarm, or filled with doubts, should once and for all leave theology alone. "The Holy Ghost is not a sceptic," he thundered forth in another place. "He has not inspired our hearts with some vague illusion, but has planted a strong certainty there." Obstinately, Luther clings to his outlook that man can only be good if he carries God in his heart, and he is bad when the Devil rides on his back; his own will remains unsubstantial, and is powerless against the inevitable and immutable prevision of God. Gradually, out of the single problem, out of this single issue, a far greater contrast arose. Like a parting of the waters, and in accordance with their temperaments, there emerges the conviction that these two renovators of religion have totally different conceptions of Christ's essence and being. For Erasmus, the humanist, Christ was the messenger of everything human, the divine being who had given His blood in order that the shedding of blood might disappear from the world, together with discord and quarrelsomeness. Luther, however, God's lansquenet, insisted on the literal rendering of the text, "I come not to send peace, but a sword." He who wishes to be a true Christian, says Erasmus, must live peacefully and act with forbearance in the spirit of the Lord Jesus. To which the inflexible Luther responded that the true Christian must never yield an inch of his ground so far as God's word is concerned even if the world should have to come to an end through his tenacity. Years before, he had written to Spalatinus: "I do not think that the cause can be carried to a successful issue without tumult, vexation, and insurrection. You cannot make a quill-pen out of a sword, nor change war into peace. God's word is war and vexation and destruction, it is poison. Like a bear in the path, like a lioness in the jungle, it attacks the sons of Ephraim." Quickly hurling Erasmus's summons to unity and understanding in his rival's teeth, Luther continued: "Let be with your complaining and clamour;

against such a fever no medicines can prevail. This war is our Lord God's war. He has unchained it, and never will it cease raging until all the enemies of His word have been wiped from the face of the earth." Erasmus's gentle and conciliatory ways "show a lack of true Christian faith"; it is, therefore, better that he stand aside and busy himself with meritorious labours, such as translating Latin and Greek texts into good German; should amuse himself with his humanistic trifling, and should desist from meddling with problems which can only be elucidated by the inner certitude of a believing, of a completely believing, mortal. Dictatorially, Erasmus was ordered once and for all to refrain from intervening in this religious struggle which by now had become a matter of worldwide importance: "God has not blessed you with strength sufficient to be of use to the cause, nor did He wish you to have such powers." He, Luther, however, felt the call, and thus his conscience gave him a sense of certainty: "What or who I am, and for what purpose and in what spirit I have become mixed in this fight, I leave to God Who knows all; that which I perform was not initiated through my will but through His divine and free will, and it is through Him that I have accomplished the tasks under my hand."

Thus was the issue between the humanists and the reformers settled. The Erasmic spirit and the Lutheran, reason versus passion, a religion of humanity as against a fanatical belief, supranationality and nationality, versatility and one-sidedness, flexibility and rigidity, all these disparate things were and are as little able to combine as fire and water. Whenever they encounter one another here below, they engender rage and wrath, setting up one element to fight the other.

Luther never forgave Erasmus the public attack the latter had made upon him. This combative man could not brook any other end to a fight than that his adversary be completely overthrown. Whereas Erasmus, once having said his say—as in *Hyperaspistes,* which for a person of his soft and yielding disposition was a fairly violent piece of writing—was content to return to his studies, Luther's hate continued to glow and increase in intensity. He never missed an opportunity for hurling insults at the man who had had the audacity to differ from him on one single point; and, in his "murderous hatred" (as Erasmus called it), he did not recoil from vilification and actual calumny. "He who crushes Erasmus cracks a bug which stinks even worse when dead than when alive." He named the scholar of Rotterdam "the fiercest of Christ's foes"; and when he was shown a portrait of Erasmus he said warningly to his friends: "This is the face of a wily and malignant man who has made mock both of God and of religion . . . who, night and day, excogitates some freshly evasive term; and if ever one fancies he has said something vital one finds on examination that he has said nothing at all." At table he apostrophized the friends assembled over meat, exclaiming furiously: "I take you all as witnesses for what I am about to declare. In my testament I mean to declare plainly that I hold Erasmus to be the greatest enemy of Christ, such an enemy as does not appear more than once in a thousand years." Moreover, he did not shrink from blasphemy: "When I pray, 'Blessed be Thy holy name,' I curse Erasmus and his heretical congeners who revile and profane God."

Nevertheless, though Luther was the man of wrath personified, though in battle his eyes became bloodshot, he was not always at war, but had, on account of his doctrine and its influence, at times to exercise the arts of diplomacy. Maybe his friends drew his attention to the fact that it was unwise to bespatter the old man with such intolerable abuse, seeing that Erasmus was esteemed and honoured throughout the length and breadth of Europe. Anyway, after a year of terrific diatribes

against this "greatest enemy of God," Luther laid the
sword aside and took an olive branch in hand, writing
an almost jovial letter wherein he excused himself for
having "dealt such hard blows." This time it was Erasmus who curtly refused to be conciliated. "I am not so
childish that, after having all imaginable abuse hurled at
me, I can be won over by jokes and flattery. . . . To
what purpose were all those mockeries and those de-
grading lies, the accusations of my being an atheist, a
sceptic in matters of faith, a blasphemer, and I know not
what besides? . . . That which has passed between us
is not important, least of all to me who am nearing my
end. But what, to every man who respects himself and
to me personally, gives cause for vexation is that, by
your immoderate, shameless, and instigatory behaviour,
you have disturbed the whole world . . . and that,
through your will, this storm cannot come to the good
end for which I have fought. . . . Our dispute is a private matter; but my heart is sorely grieved at the widespread suffering and the incurable confusion, for which
we have no one to thank but yourself, with your unbridled ways, and the impossibility of getting you to
follow good counsel. . . . I could have wished you to
possess another kind of mentality than the one you possess, the one you admire so greatly. You may wish me

anything you like with the exception of this mentality of yours. May the Lord intervene to change it!"

Thus, with a harshness quite foreign to his nature, Erasmus rejected the overtures to peace, refused to shake the hand which had laid his universe to waste. He refused to know Luther or to greet Luther any more, for the peace of the Church had been destroyed by this violent man who had provoked the most appalling "tumultus" of the spirit, and had let slip the dogs of war in Germany and the entire world.

But tumult raged throughout the lands, and no one could evade it, not even Erasmus. Unrest became the law of the day, and fate had decreed that whenever Erasmus longed for rest the world rose against him to prevent it. Basle, the town to which he had fled because of its neutrality, was gripped in the fever of the Reformation. The mob stormed churches, tore down pictures from the altars and statues from their niches, and burned the lot in three separate heaps in the minster square. Erasmus saw his perennial enemy, fanaticism, raging round his home with firebrand and sword. One small consolation remained to him, that in the course of the tumult no blood was shed. "Would that it could always be thus!"

Now that Basle had taken a firm stand in favour of the Reformation and had espoused one side of the dispute to the exclusion of the other, it was no longer the asylum Erasmus needed for his peace of mind. He felt that he could not remain within its walls. At sixty years of age, Erasmus transferred his home to the quiet little town of Freiburg-im-Breisgau (then Austrian), so that he might carry on his work in tranquillity. He was met by a solemn procession of burghers and officials, who presented him with a veritable palace as place of habitation. He declined this magnificent offer, preferring to instal himself in more modest quarters next door to the monastery where he hoped to continue his studies and end his days in peace and quiet. History could have furnished no better symbol for a man who kept to the golden mean, who was on intimate terms with no one because he was incapable of taking sides: Erasmus was forced to leave Louvain because it was too Catholic; he was forced to leave Basle because it was too Protestant. A free and independent mind, which refuses to be bound by any dogma and declines to join any party, never finds a home upon this earth.

THE END

ERASMUS was sixty years of age; he was weary and worn out. Once again, this time in Freiburg, he sat behind his books, a fugitive—how many times before had he played the same role?—a fugitive from the rush and turmoil of the world. His delicate frame seemed to shrink in size as the years sped by, his sensitive face with its network of wrinkles and folds came increasingly to resemble a parchment inscribed with mystic runes and ciphers. He who had so implicitly believed in the possibility of a resurrection and renovation of man and his world by the workings of the spirit and the mind grew bitterer, more mocking, and more ironical in his attitude to the world without. Peevish and crabbed of temper like all confirmed bachelors, he complained ceaselessly of the decay of scientific culture, lamented that his foes had such reserves of hate to draw upon, grumbled about the costliness of living and bemoaned the trickiness of bankers, was quer-

ulous concerning the quality of the wines he drank. Increasingly disappointed, Erasmus withdrew from a
world estranged, a world which refused to keep the
peace, a world which had slain reason by means of passion, and justice by means of violence. His heart was
drowsy, but his hand was as vigorous as ever, his mind
as keen and bright as a lamp shedding immaculate rays
in a wide circle about it, and penetrating to the remotest
corners of the field of vision his incorruptible intelligence
surveyed. One friend alone, his oldest, best, and trust-
worthiest friend, shared study and writing-table with
him: Dame Work. Each day he wrote thirty to forty
letters, he filled folio after folio of translations from the
Fathers, he added to his *Colloquia*, and composed innumerable works dealing with morals and æsthetics. He
wrote and wrought with the consciousness of a man
who believed in the right and the duty of reason, and
who had set himself the task of announcing its undying
truth to a thankless world. But in his heart of hearts he
knew that it was useless to issue a summons to a higher
humanity in troublous times, when men had gone mad;
he realized that his sublime idea of humanism was a
pricked bubble. Everything he had longed for, had
fought for—mutual understanding and kindly conciliation in the place of savage warfare—had been ship-

wrecked upon the shoals of zealotry and stubbornness; his spiritual realm, his Platonic State, which was to have been established in the midst of the earthly world about him, his republic of scholars, all this could find no place on the battlefields where the parties and factions were fighting. Between Germany and France and Italy and Spain, campaigns were ceaselessly carried on, and vast armies like wandering thunderstorms ravened across these unhappy lands; Christ's name had become a war-cry and a standard around which forgathered the military activity of the day. How absurd to go on writing tracts and to beseech the princes to come to their senses, how unreasonable to continue being the advocate of evangelical teachings since God's representative and messenger had taken the word "Evangel" to serve as a bone of contention. "These words 'Evangel,' 'God's truth,' 'faith,' 'Christ,' 'spirit,' are perpetually spilling from their mouths, and yet I see many of them so conducting themselves as if they were possessed of the devil." No, it was most decidedly a waste of time and trouble to try, in an epoch of political turmoil, to act as mediator and to compose differences. The exalted dream of a spiritually united, humanistic Europe had come to an end; and he who had dreamed this dream, Erasmus, now a tired old man, was no longer of any use, for no one hearkened to his message. The world of men passed him by; he was not needed now.

Nevertheless, before a candle goes out, it flutters up into a sturdy flame. Before an idea can be quenched in the storms of an epoch, it has one last flicker of energy. Thus it was with Erasmus. Short-lived but magnificent, the Erasmic thought, the idea of reconciliation and conciliation, flamed anew. Charles V, ruler of two worlds, came to a momentous decision. He was no longer the timid boy he had been at the time of his coronation and at the Diet of Worms. Disappointment and experience had schooled and matured him, and the splendid victory he had just achieved over France provided him with what he lacked in the way of self-confidence and authority. On his return to Germany after the campaign, he resolved to put order into the religious chaos, to reinstate the unity of the Church so wantonly destroyed by Luther, and to do so even if he had to resort to force. But before using force he determined to set about the task in the Erasmic way, by endeavouring to bring the contending parties to an agreement, to create a modus vivendi between the old-established Church and the new ideas, to "summon a council of wise and unprejudiced men," so that they might in Christian love and

[224]

charity listen to every argument, and select those points which could serve as foundation for a united and renewed Christian Church. With this goal in view, Emperor Charles V called the Diet of Augsburg.

The Diet of Augsburg proved to be one of the most momentous events in the history of the German people, and, indeed, in the history of the world, one of those events that can never recur and which are pregnant with possibilities for the coming centuries. To outward appearance, the Diet of Augsburg was less dramatic than that held at Worms some years previously, but it certainly does not lag behind the earlier one as far as its lasting historical importance is concerned. Now, as then, the point at issue was the spiritual and intellectual unity of the western world.

At the outset, the Diet of Augsburg was extraordinarily favourable to the Erasmic idea, that of a conciliatory discussion between the opponents. Both parties to the dispute, the old Church and the new, were going through a severe crisis, and were, therefore, ripe for an understanding. The Catholic Church had lost much of its former arrogance, and no longer looked disdainfully down upon "the insignificant German heretic," for she realized that the Reformation movement had kindled a blaze throughout northern Europe, a conflagration

[225]

which was spreading farther and farther over the land. The Netherlands, Sweden, Switzerland, Denmark, and (this was the cruellest blow) England had gone over to the new doctrines; everywhere the penurious rulers were realizing how conveniently they could fill their treasuries by closing down the religious establishments and confiscating ecclesiastical possessions in the name of Holy Writ. The ancient weapons of Mother Church, excommunication, exorcism, and the like, did not impose upon people now as in the days of Canossa, for had not an Augustinian monk of no importance defied the papal ban and burned the bull cheerfully in a public bonfire? But where the papacy had suffered most was in its self-esteem; wounded to the heart it had to contemplate its ravaged estates from the heights of the Holy See. The "sacco di Roma" had ruined the prestige of the curia for decades to come.

Luther, too, and his followers had gone through much trial and tribulation since the exciting and heroic days at Worms. In the evangelical camp, likewise, "the loving concord of the Church" had been rent and torn. Ere Luther had been given time to organize a compact congregation of the faithful, rivals had entered the field. There were Zwingli and Karlstadt and Henry VIII and the sects of the zealots and the Anabaptists to contend with. This fanatical believer had come to realize that what he desired to establish on the spiritual plane was being interpreted in the material sense, was being exploited for utilitarian purposes and for personal advantage. Gustav Freytag has given apt expression to the tragedy which brooded over Luther's life in later years. "He who is destined to create the greatest thing imaginable has at one and the same time to tear into shreds a part of his own life. The more conscientiously he sets himself to the task, the more acutely does he feel within his own heart the cleavage he has brought into the ordering of the world. This is the hidden wound, aye, the feeling of compunction, which invariably accompanies every world-shaking thought." For the first time this hard and irreconcilable creature showed an inclination towards understanding; his followers, too, were more cautious since they observed that their overlord and emperor Charles V had freed his arms and was ready once again to wield his trusty blade. Many of them were thinking that it might be advisable not to stand as rebels before their liege lord, who was also the master of Europe. One's lands and one's head might easily pay the forfeit for any sign of opposition.

At length the terrible obstinacy of both sides was broken, that inflexible and unyielding stubbornness which characterized the fight in Germany before and after the Diet of Augsburg. Should a reconciliation in the Erasmic spirit be brought about, should the old Church and the new come to an agreement, then Germany and indeed the whole world would once again be united, and the period of religious warfare and of civil strife could be ended for ever. The moral overlordship of Germany would be securely established, and the disgraceful religious persecutions would cease. No longer would people be burned at the stake on account of their opinions; the Index and the Inquisition need no longer set their baleful stigma upon the freedom of the mind; and Europe would henceforward be spared immeasurable wretchedness. The opponents were separated by such a small bridge now. Would they cross it? Just a little give and take on both sides, and reason, humanism, the Erasmic concept, would gain the day.

A promising sign in the encounter was that this time the evangelical cause was not in Luther's ruthless hands but was to be pleaded by the more diplomatic Melanchthon. This extraordinarily gentle and noble-minded man, honoured by the Protestant Church as the truest friend and assistant Luther ever had, remained all his life the faithful disciple of Erasmus. His whole nature, his attitude of mind throughout the conflict, made him sympathetic to the humanistic and humane ideas of Luther's most formidable opponent, and his concept of evangelical teaching ran better in harness with Erasmus's than with the less malleable and severer formula of Luther. But nevertheless Luther's personality and strength worked suggestively upon Melanchthon. In Wittenberg, in Luther's immediate neighbourhood, Melanchthon felt himself completely subservient to Luther's will; he served the master humbly and with all the zeal his clear-thinking and organizing mind was capable of. In Augsburg, however, away from the hypnotic influence of the master, the other side, the Erasmic side of Melanchthon's nature, could be given free play. During the diet at Augsburg he went out of his way to be conciliatory, going so far in his concessions that his feet almost led him back into the fold of Roman communion. He himself was responsible for the "Augsburg Confession." Luther could never "have trod so softly and gently." This document, in spite of its unambiguous and artistic phraseology, was in no way provocative and could not wound the pride of the Catholic Church. During the discussions, too, many highly controversial points were passed over in silence. Thus, the doctrine of predestination, about which Luther and Erasmus had fought so bitterly, was not referred to, nor was the

thorny problem of the divine right of the papacy mentioned, nor the "character indelebilis," the inalienable
quality of priesthood, nor the seven sacraments. From
either side conciliatory words were spoken. Melanchthon wrote: "We respect the authority of the pope and
the Church so long as the pope of Rome refrains from
casting us out." A representative of the Vatican, on the
other hand, made a semi-official declaration that such
questions as the celibacy of the clergy and lay communion in both kinds were "discutable." The assembly,
in spite of untold difficulties, was beginning to hope;
and if a man of high moral authority, a man possessing
a profound and passionate will to peace, had been at
hand to put his whole weight, his full eloquence, all the
logic at his command, into the scale on the side of reconciliation, who knows but that at the eleventh hour
Protestants and Catholics, the parties with both of
which he was closely associated (the former by sympathy and the latter by fidelity), might not have been
brought to a unity which would have saved the ideal of
a united European Christendom?

The only man then living who might have brought
this miracle to pass was Erasmus, and Emperor Charles
V, the ruler of two worlds, had sent him a special invitation to be present at the diet, conjuring him to give

advice and to act as mediator. But Erasmus's tragic destiny recapitulated itself. Again, as so often before, he missed a magnificent and unique opportunity because of overcautiousness, because of his innate weakness and his incapacity for coming to a definite conclusion. What had happened at the Diet of Worms happened again now. Erasmus failed to put in an appearance. He could not bring himself to stand firm on a vital issue, to risk his person for his faith. Granted, he wrote letters, many letters to both parties, very shrewd, very human, very convincing letters; he sought out his friends in both camps, Melanchthon in one and the papal representative in the other, beseeching them to shed their extremer differences and meet half-way. But the written word has never, in times of tension and doom, the strength of warm and living speech, the vocal call to arms. Luther, too, sent message after message from his retreat in Co burg, endeavouring to render Melanchthon stiffer than he was by nature and inclination. In the end the contrasts became acute once more because the right man, the man of genial and conciliatory habit, was lacking. Discussion followed upon discussion, and the idea of conciliation was ground between the upper and the nether millstones of the old and the new Church. The Diet of Augsburg rent Christendom in twain, and yet it had been summoned with a view to bringing the parties together in a spirit of concord. Henceforward there were to be two faiths, and instead of peace the world knew only strife. Luther harshly drew his conclusions: "If war comes of it, very well then, war will come; but we have done all we could to avoid it." And Erasmus tragically observes: "If a terrible confusion floods our world, remember that Erasmus foretold its advent."

From those momentous days onward, the Erasmic idea was dead. The old man behind his barricade of books in Freiburg was nothing but a useless bag of bones, and enjoyed the merest shadow of his former fame. He himself considered it to be better for a man who felt at home only in the realm of calm forbearance to withdraw from "this noisy, or, better said, crazy epoch." Why should he continue to drag his frail and sickly carcass about a world inimical and estranged? Erasmus was weary of the life he had once loved so well. We are shaken profoundly when we read his plaintive prayer, "May God gather me soon unto Himself so that I quit this mad world." For where had the spirit room to live and to grow, now that fanaticism raged through the land? The sublime realm of humanism which Erasmus had built had been overrun by enemy hordes and wellnigh conquered; gone were the days of "eruditio et eloquentia"; men no longer hearkened to the subtle and delicate message of imaginative genius, but turned their ears to listen to the rough and passion-wrought babble of politics. Thought had succumbed to mob-frenzy, it had donned the uniform of Luther or of the pope; the erudite no longer waged war in elegantly phrased epistles and books, but, like fishwives, hurled gross invectives at each other's heads; none was willing to understand what his neighbour said, but instead each tried to impose his own pet belief, his particular doctrine, upon all the rest. Woe unto him who stood aside and took no part in the game! Twofold hatred was hurled against those who remained aloof. Those who live for the spirit are lonely indeed at times when passion rages. Who is there left to write for when ears are deafened with political yappings and yelpings? Delicate tones of irony pass unheeded, and subtle points of theology can no longer be discussed with people who use cannon and soldiery for arguments. A pack of hounds had been let loose upon those whose opinions differed from one's own, upon those of independent mind. Christianity was to be served with caltrops and the executioner's sword; even men of intellect and culture, even the sturdiest and most honest believer, seized upon the roughest methods

to impose their will. Tumult had come with a venge-
ance! From every land came tidings that pricked Erasmus to the heart. Berquin, his translator and pupil, had
been strangled and his body burned; in England, his
beloved John Fisher and Thomas More, the noblest of
his friends, had perished on the scaffold (Blessed be they
who possess strength enough to give their lives for the
faith!). On receiving the news, Erasmus groaned: "Me-
thinks 'tis I myself who have died." Zwingli, with
whom he had exchanged so many letters and friendly
words, was slain on the battlefield at Kappel; Thomas
Münzer was done to death with tortures which even the
heathen or the Chinese could not have made more horrible. Anabaptists had their tongues torn out, the itiner-
ant preachers were flayed alive and burned at the stake,
churches were plundered, books destroyed in the
flames, cities and towns were razed to the ground,
Rome, the glory of the world, was sacked—oh, God,
what bestial excesses are committed in Thy name! Verily the world had no room for freedom of thought, for
understanding and consideration, these fundamental
tenets of the humanistic doctrine. Art could not flourish
on so blood-drenched a soil; for decades, for centuries,
perhaps for ever were gone the days of supranational
community; even Latin, the language of a united Eu-

rope, the language of Erasmus's very heart, was dead.
Die thou, likewise, Erasmus!

Fate pursued him to the end. The wanderer had
again, for a last time, to betake himself to the road. Close
on seventy, Erasmus left his house and home. An inexplicable yearning had seized him to forsake Freiburg
and journey to Brabant. The duke had invited him to
come, but in reality another summoned him: Death.
Erasmus was prey to a strange restlessness of soul. He
who all his life had been a pilgrim in many lands, who
had been a cosmopolitan, who had deliberately re-
nounced his fatherland, of a sudden felt the need to
tread for a last time the soil of his native country. His
tired body longed to return whence it had come; he had
a premonition that the end was near.

He was destined never to reach his goal. In a tiny
postchaise, the kind that was usually employed for conveying women, he drove to Basle. The old man thought
to remain there only until the ice broke and then, in the
springtime, to voyage down the Rhine to the land of
his birth. Meanwhile, Basle put its spell upon him. Here
he felt a spiritual and intellectual warmth encompassing
him, here a few staunch friends lived, Frobenius's son,
Amerbach, and others. They saw to it that the invalid

was made comfortable; he was housed among them. Also there was still the printing-house where he could once again see his thoughts reflected upon the printed page, where he could breathe the atmosphere of ink, where he could handle the exquisitely printed books, where he could sit in silent colloquy with the beautiful, peaceful, and informative works of the masters. In tranquil retirement, away from the noise and bustle of the world, too weary and sapless to leave his bed for more than four or five hours out of the twenty-four, Erasmus passed his last days. His heart seemed frozen, he felt that he was forgotten or despised, for the Catholics no longer wooed his favours and the Protestants made mock of him. No one needed him; no one asked his opinion, no one hung upon his words. "My foes increase in number, while my friends become fewer," he wailed despairingly in his solitude, he for whom urbane spiritual converse had been the acme of life's beauty and happiness.

But lo, like a belated swallow, someone came knocking at his window already frosted by the cold of approaching winter. A message flew in to greet him with reverence and love. "Everything that I do, all that I am, I owe to you; and, were I to fail in acknowledging my debt, I should prove the most ungrateful man alive.

Salve itaque etiam atque etiam, pater amantissime, pater desusque patriæ, literarum assertor, veritatis propugnator invictissime." (Greeting and yet again greeting, dearest father and honour of the land which gave you birth, champion of the arts, invincible fighter for truth.) The name of the man who wrote these words, and one which was destined to outshine even the name of Erasmus, was Rabelais, who in the dawn of his youthful glory thus acclaimed the dying master whose sun was about to set. There followed yet another letter, a letter from Rome. Impatiently, Erasmus broke the seals. Then a bitter laugh issued from between his thin lips as he let the missive drop from his hand. Was he not being made mock of? The new pope was offering him a cardinal's hat, a post that was lucrative, to him who had his life long refused all situations which might curtail his intellectual independence. Proudly he laid the almost galling honour aside. "Shall I, a dying man, burden myself with something which I have hitherto invariably refused to shoulder?" No, he must die a free man as he had lived a free man. Free, dressed as a burgher, without decorations and mundane honours, free as are all solitaries, and alone as are all the free spirits of this world.

The truest friend of the solitary, one who never quits

his side, one who is always ready to act as comforter, Dame Work, she remained with Erasmus to the last. His body tortured with sickness, lying for the most part in bed, his hand trembling with weakness and age, he wrote and wrote, day in day out, composing his commentary on Origen, sending off letters, preparing pamphlets for the press. No longer was he writing for celebrity's sake, nor was it for money that he laboured, but simply and solely for the secret pleasure of learning by spiritualizing life, and, by learning, to strengthen his own life. To inhale knowledge and to exhale it, this eternal systole and diastole of earthly existence, only this circle of movement and activity kept his blood aflow. Toiling to the last, he fled from the real world through the sacred groves and labyrinths of work, away from the world which no longer recognized him or understood him, from the world which had no desire even to recognize him or understand him. In due course the Bringer of Peace stood at his bedside, and, now that death was so close upon him, Erasmus, who had always dreaded his advent, looked up at him calmly and almost gratefully. His mind remained clear to the last, he compared the friends gathered about him, Frobenius and Amerbach, with Job's comforters, conversing with them in witty and elegant Latin. Just before the end, when the death-rattle was already heard in his throat, a strange thing happened. He who had always spoken Latin and thought and written in Latin, suddenly forgot that tongue, and, with the primitive fear of the animal upon him, he stammered out the words he had learned in earliest childhood, "lieve God"—the first words and the last words Erasmus ever spoke were in the Teutonic vernacular. One more breath, and then he got what he had longed that all humanity should receive—Peace.

ERASMUS'S LEGACY

AT the very time when Erasmus, on his death-
bed, bequeathed his spiritual inheritance of
European unity as the sublimest ideal to coming generations, there appeared in Florence one of the most
momentous books the world had ever seen. This was
the famous work by Niccolò Machiavelli, entitled *Il
Principe*. In this mathematically clear textbook of the
ruthless exercise of power and conquest in the realm of
politics, we find the counterpoise to Erasmus's teaching plainly set forth and formulated as if in a catechism.
While Erasmus demanded that princes and peoples
should freely and peaceably subordinate their personal,
their egoistic, their imperialistic claims to a fraternal
commonwealth of the whole of mankind, Machiavelli
belauded the will to power of every prince, acclaiming
this as the highest and as the only aim of every nation.
All the forces of the commonalty should, he maintained, be made to serve the folk-idea with as much

devotion as though it were a religious idea; the "raison d'état," the utmost development of the individuality, must become the only visible object and goal of historical evolution, and their ruthless achievement must be looked upon as the sublimest duty within the orbit of world occurrences. For Machiavelli, power and the development of power were the ultimate expression of the individual or the collective personality; for Erasmus it was justice.

Thus, for all time, the two great fundamental forms of world politics were given their intellectual shape, the practical as against the ideal, diplomacy as against ethics, State politics as against humane politics. Erasmus, the philosopher contemplating the world, held, as did Aristotle, Plato, and Thomas Aquinas, that politics should be placed in the same category as ethics; a prince, as the leader of the State, should first of all be the servant of the divine, the exponent of the ethical ideal. Machiavelli, with the practical experience of a diplomatist, made politics an amoral and independent science, saying that they had as little to do with ethics as had astronomy and geometry. A prince, or a leader of a State, had no business to be dreaming dreams about humanity, that vague and intangible concept, but should reckon quite unsentimentally with men as the only concrete

material which should be utilized with all its forces
and its weaknesses to the personal advancement of
the prince and of the nation he governed. Clearly
and coldly, with as little consideration as a chess-player
towards his partner, a prince should go his way, and
by every means, permissible and unpermissible, ensure
the utmost advantage and dominion for his own people.
Power and expansion of power were for Machiavelli
the supremest duty, and success the decisive justification of both prince and people.

In the material realm of history the principle of
power has achieved a predominant position. Not so
Erasmus's ideal of politics based upon conciliation and
the unity of mankind. The concepts set forth in *Il Principe* have held the field, the policy of seizing every opportunity to reinforce the personal power of a sovereign
has presided over the dramatic development of European history, ever since that day. Generations of diplo-
mats have drunk at the spring tapped by the terribly
keen-minded Florentine. The barriers between nations
have been built of blood and iron, barriers for ever
shifting and changing. Conflict instead of community
of interests has made good its claim to monopolize the
best energies of the European peoples. Never has Erasmus's thought taken sufficient shape and substance to

exercise a tangible influence upon the moulding of European destinies. The great humanistic dream of the solution of disagreements in a spirit of justice, the longed-for unification of the nations under the ægis of a common culture, has remained a Utopia, never yet established, and, maybe, impossible of achievement within the domain of reality.

Nevertheless, in the realm of mind there is room for every kind of contrast. Even that which in the concrete world can never be victorious remains in that other as a dynamic force, and unfulfilled ideals often prove the most unconquerable. An idea which does not take on material shape is not necessarily a conquered idea or a false idea; it may represent a need which, though its gratification be postponed, is and remains a need. Nay, more: an ideal which, because it has failed to secure embodiment in action, is neither worn out nor compromised in any way, continues to work as a ferment in subsequent generations, urging them to the achievement of a higher morality. Those ideals only which have failed to put on concrete form are capable of everlasting resurrection.

In the mental sphere, therefore, the humanistic ideal, Erasmus's ideal, the first visible effort to bring about European unity, has suffered no depreciation because it

failed to achieve dominion and wielded hardly any political power. The essence of volition is not to be above
party, but invariably to be biased and to belong to a
majority. We can harbour only a very faint hope that
the calm and composure of mind which Goethe held to
be the holiest and sublimest form of life will ever take
shape and content in the soul of the masses of mankind.
The humanistic ideal, that ideal grounded upon breadth
of vision and clarity of mind, is destined to remain a
spiritual and aristocratic dream which few mortals are
capable of dreaming, but which those few inherit as a
sacred legacy held in trust for others who shall come
after and be handed down from one generation to the
next. The idea of a future when all mankind shall work
harmoniously together towards a common destiny has
never, even during the darkest hours of European history, been utterly lost sight of.

Erasmus, that disappointed old man who nonetheless
was never disappointed, labouring in the midst of the
warring nations and a Europe ravaged and laid waste,
collected the materials of a legacy which was nothing
other than the ancient dream of every religion, of every
myth, the dream of a coming and irresistible humaniza-
tion of mankind, of a triumph of the unclouded and
just-minded reason over selfish and ephemeral passions.

Though his hand was unsure and often hesitant, Erasmus was the first to give this ideal a practical shape, and this ideal has been looked up to with hope renewed by all the generations of Europeans which have arisen since his day. No thought that is the outcome of the fusion of clear thinking with high moral energy can wholly disappear; even though the hand may falter and the structure be incomplete, the ethical spirit will shape it anew. Erasmus, the conquered, has earned his fame here below because he broke trail in the world of literature for humanistic ideals. It is to him we owe this simplest of thoughts, and this most undying of thoughts, namely, that it is mankind's highest duty to seek to become humaner, more spiritual, and increasingly capable of sympathetic, of spiritual, understanding. Montaigne, who looked upon "inhumaneness as the worst of all burdens," declaring it something "que ie n'ay point le courage de concevoir sans horreur," continued to preach the message of comprehension and forbearance his master, Erasmus, had launched upon the world. Spinoza demanded that, instead of being guided by blind passion, men should, rather, look to the "amor intellectualis"; Diderot, Voltaire, and Lessing, sceptics and idealists at one and the same time, were continually at war against narrow-mindedness and bigotry, advocating in their stead "a tolerance full of understanding." Schiller gave the message of world-citizenship a poetic dress; Kant demanded everlasting peace; again and again, down to the days of Tolstoy, and now with Gandhi and Romain Rolland, this same ideal has been reiterated with logical force, and the spirit of understanding has claimed its ethical and moral rights as a counterblast to the club-law of authority and violence.

With faith ever freshly renewed, men still look to the possibility of a reconciliation between the nations, and the hope arises all the stronger in the human heart precisely at those moments when confusion and horror are abroad in the land. For man cannot live and work without the comforting delusion that humanity is really capable of rising to a higher moral plane, without his dream that in the end he and his fellow-mortals will be reconciled and will understand one another. And though there are shrewd and calculating persons who maintain that the fulfilment of the Erasmic dream is out of the question, and although the present trend of things may seem to show that they are right, nevertheless, such "hard-headed and practical" persons must again and again be reminded that there exist bonds as well as bar-riers between the nations, and that in the hearts of men the ardent hopes of a coming age when a higher humanity will exist are unceasingly renewed. A promise is thus contained within the legacy, a promise which is full of creative force for the future. For what the mind is capable of lifting from the narrow circle of the individual life and hurling forth into the realm of the universally human, that alone is capable of endowing us with strength beyond the strength of the individual. Men and nations can find their true and sacred measure only by making suprapersonal and hardly realizable claims.